Gotham in

For Ellie,
With our thanks,
D Ow Dp

Glory in Gotham

Manhattan's Houses of Worship

A Guide to Their History, Architecture and Legacy

David W. Dunlap
and
Joseph J. Vecchione

Photographs by David W. Dunlap

A CITY & COMPANY GUIDE

Library of Congress Cataloging-in-Publication Date
is available upon request.
First Edition
ISBN 1-929439-01-6
Printed in the United States of America

10 9 8 7 6 5 4 3 2 1

Acknowledgements

We had good company on our journey through civic history, liturgical art and architecture, and New York's many vibrant communities of faith, but we are especially indebted to those colleagues and friends who reviewed and edited the manuscript and provided clear direction and sound counsel: Robert Braham, Laura M. Chmielewski, William G. Connolly, Andrew Scott Dolkart, Christopher Gray, Holly Kaye, Michael J. Leahy, Ken Lustbader, Laurie Marcus, the Rev. Richard R. McKeon, Rosalie R. Radomsky, the Rt. Rev. Catherine S. Roskam, Mervyn Rothstein, Joseph P. Sullivan and Stephen Wagley.

Invaluable assistance and information were offered generously by Lisa Anderson, Cary Bernstein, the Rev. Dr. Paul W. Brouse Jr., Mary Ellen Burgess, the Rev. Earl Cooperkamp, Terri Rosen Deutsch, Major David Dlugose, Erica Espinal, Craig Evans, Douglas Franklin, Rabbi Jonathan Wilson Glass, Ruchie Glattstein, David Gonzalez, Joe Guenther, Linda Hall, Bob Hemans, Neville Hughes, the Rev. Brenda G. Husson, Stephen Jacobs, Winston James, the Rev. David Johnson, Herb Katz, Father Leonid Kishkovsky, Father Karl Krauser, the Rev. Peter Laarman, Alexis Liberovsky, Rabbi David H. Lincoln, the Rev. Matthew Lui, the Rev. O'Neil Mackey, Jim McGrath,

Dorothy McWhite, Marty Michael,
the Rev. Panczyk Mirek, Dabney Montgomery,
Cara Moore, Jack Morris, Jennifer Oetting,
Al Orensanz, Beverly Pena, Pastor Neil Rhodes,
Hilda Rodriguez, Mark Rosenzweig, Jeff Roth,
Serge Schmemann, Linda Sheean, Jessica Silver,
Julie L. Sloan, Rabbi Kenneth Stern, Edgar Tafel,
Rabbi Noach Valley, Darren Walker,
Kristin Walsh, Amy Waterman, Craig Whitney,
Elder Donovan Williams, the Rev. Steven Woolly
and Yin Liang.

Helene Silver and Melisa Coburn of City &
Company welcomed the proposal and
nurtured it wisely. Toula Ballas and
Rebekka Linton strengthened our text considerably by their editing, Don Wise set it off in
a handsome design and John Papasian
complemented it with his terrifically detailed
maps. The prints were made at Modernage
Custom Imaging Labs and Time-Life
Photographic Laboratories.

Our real partners in the project—sustaining,
supportive and supremely patient—were
Elizabeth Vecchione and Scott Bane, to whom
we owe the greatest debt of gratitude.

Contents by Neighborhood

Lincoln Center and Vicinity 95

Upper West Side and Morningside Heights 105

Upper East Side and Yorkville 121

Harlem, El Barrio and Upper Manhattan 143

Contents by Denomination

Russian Orthodox

St. Nicholas Russian
  Orthodox Cathedral 138

Salvation Army

Salvation Army Centennial
  Memorial Chapel 68

Serbian Orthodox

St. Sava Serbian Orthodox
  Cathedral 67

Ukrainian Catholic

St. George Ukrainian
  Catholic Church 56

Unitarian Universalist

All Souls Church 122
Fourth Universalist Society 110

United Church of Christ

Judson Memorial Church 53
Riverside Church 112

Secular

Angel Orensanz Foundation 32
The Cloisters 148
John's Pizzeria 81
Limelight 63
Portico Place Apartments 55

Introduction

Three and a half centuries of spiritual journeying on Manhattan Island have left an extraordinary social, artistic and architectural legacy: more than 100 buildings that would easily earn two or three stars on, say, a European itinerary. Unfortunately, few New Yorkers and even fewer visitors focus on these cultural and historical treasures, whose variety alone is surely unrivaled in any other city. *Glory in Gotham: Manhattan's Houses of Worship* is an invitation to explore and celebrate the transcendent qualities that recommend these fascinating places to anyone, regardless of faith (or lack thereof). You don't have to be Jewish to marvel at Temple Emanu-El, the world's largest synagogue, or to be moved by the artistry and abandonment of the Eldridge Street Synagogue. You don't have to be Episcopalian to feel awestruck by the brooding majesty of the Cathedral Church of St. John the Divine. Nor is an understanding of Slavonic required to delight in the onion domes of St. Nicholas Russian Orthodox Cathedral. You don't have to be Lutheran to enjoy a jazz vespers at St. Peter's or Roman Catholic to thrill at the mighty sound of the Mander organ at St. Ignatius Loyola. And a Baptist upbringing is certainly not required to catch the exuberant spirituality of Abyssinian's gospel choir. The last ecumenical overview of the city, Jonathan Greenleaf's *History of the Churches of All Denominations in the City of New York,* was published in 1846. It's time to try again. The public dialogue over the role of religion in civic life has grown considerably of late, as has the popular interest in spiritual quests. Dozens of the most significant houses of worship in New York City have been designated as official landmarks, and many of these have been restored, in part with the assistance of the Sacred Sites Program of the New York Landmarks Conservancy. A happy few even find themselves operating beyond the capacity imagined by their builders. Yet a cloud hangs over other beautiful buildings that are vastly larger than needed by the congregations that now use them. They greatly tax their members' ability to pay for basic upkeep, much less roof repair or stained-glass conservation. At the end of the 20th century, it had been more than a decade since the demolition of any   significant house of worship in Manhattan, but there is no reason to believe that all of these glorious buildings will survive. So it seems timely to chronicle them. This is not meant to be a comprehensive compilation. Rather, we've chosen institutions that are notable for their art and architecture; for their narratives and sagas; for their presence on the civic and social scenes; and for the members of the clergy who've molded and guided them. We've tried to ensure that all kinds of denominations, populations, neighborhoods and eras are represented. And who are we to do so? Not historians or theologians but two New Yorkers who've spent a combined total of 65 years in the newspaper business, which has afforded us the privilege of indulging our curiosity about our city. We've been exploring houses of worship for a decade, and the end result of that research will be a more encyclopedic work, *From Abyssinian to Zion*, to be published by Columbia University Press in 2002. Meanwhile, we take pleasure in sharing with you some of the glorious places we've found.

David W. Dunlap
Joseph J. Vecchione
New York City, December 2000

How to Use this Book

We have organized the entries in 10 broad geographic areas, from one end of the island to the other, to make it easier for you to devise your own tours; either walking or just sitting and reading. Within each area, individual houses of worship are listed alphabetically by their proper name. In other words, the Church of the Transfiguration is alphabetized as "T" not "C". Each entry denotes whether the house of worship is an official landmark—designated by the Landmarks Preservation Commission for its special historical, cultural or aesthetic value—or is within a historic district, designated by the commission as having a special sense of place as a result of its history or architecture.

An Internet address is given for institutions that maintain their own Web sites or are the subject of useful independent coverage. For example, several entries cite Web pages compiled for the class "Introduction to Medieval History," taught by Paul Halsall at Fordham University (www.fordham. edu/halsall/medny). Some addresses may be defunct by the time you read this, while other congregations will have launched their own Web sites. In some cases where there is no Web site, we have given an e-mail address.

Service information is provided for two reasons: as a guide for those who are seeking a place to worship and also as an aid to those who simply want to see the inside of the sanctuary. A number of larger institutions are open throughout the day but most sanctuaries are closed except during services. We have found, however, that an inquiry at the office can often yield a generous invitation to step inside.

At the end of each geographic area will be found a handful of other buildings that are particularly noteworthy. But don't stop at our list. The joy of this journey is discovery.

Lower Manhattan

Wall Street, the Financial District and Tribeca

1 Civic Center Synagogue
2 John Street Church
3 Shrine of St. Elizabeth Ann Seton
4 St. Paul's Chapel
5 St. Peter's Church
6 Trinity Church

Chinatown, Little Italy and the Lower East Side

7 Angel Orensanz Foundation
8 Congregation Beth Hamedrash Hagodol
9 Bialystoker Synagogue
10 Eldridge Street Synagogue
11 First Chinese Presbyterian Church
12 Mariners' Temple Baptist Church
13 St. Augustine's Church
14 St. James Church
15 St. Patrick's Old Cathedral
16 Shtiebl Row
17 Sung Tak Buddhist Association
18 Church of the Transfiguration

Greenwich Village and the East Village

19 Church of the Ascension
20 First Presbyterian Church
21 Grace Church
22 Judson Memorial Church
23 Church of Our Lady of Pompei
24 Portico Place
25 St. George Ukrainian Catholic Church
26 St. John Lutheran
27 Church of St. Luke in the Fields
28 St. Mark's Church in-the-Bowery

Chelsea, Madison Square and Vicinity

29 Church of the Holy Apostles
30 Limelight
31 Marble Collegiate Church
32 Church of Our Lady of Guadalupe
33 Church of St. Francis Xavier
34 St. Sava Serbian Orthodox Cathedral
35 Salvation Army Centennial Memorial Chapel
36 Church of the Transfiguration

Gramercy Park, Stuyvesant Square and Kips Bay

37 Brotherhood Synagogue
38 Fifteenth Street Friends Meeting House
39 St. George's Church
40 St. Vartan Armenian Cathedral

Midtown, Times Square and Clinton

41 Central Synagogue
42 Congregation Ezrath Israel
43 Fifth Avenue Presbyterian Church
44 John's Pizzeria
45 Church of St. Agnes
46 St. Bartholomew's Church
47 Church of SS. Cyril and Methodius/St. Raphael's Church
48 St. Malachy's Church
49 Church of St. Mary the Virgin
50 St. Patrick's Cathedral
51 St. Peter's Church
52 St. Thomas Church
53 Times Square Church

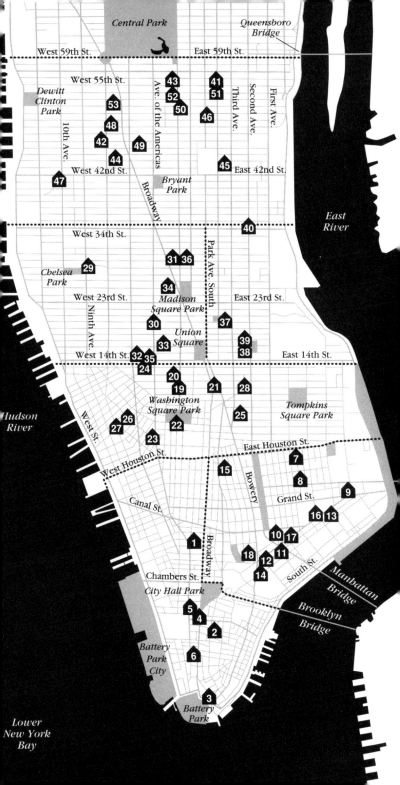

Upper Manhattan

Wall Street, the Financial District and Tribeca

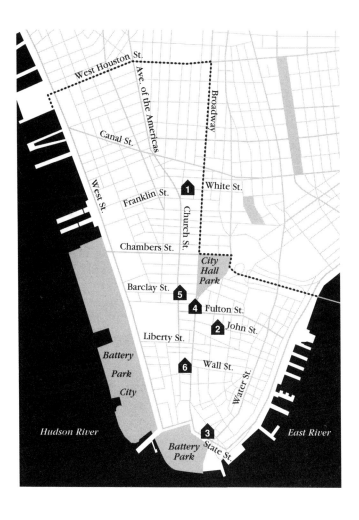

1 Civic Center Synagogue
2 John Street Church
3 Shrine of St. Elizabeth
Ann Seton

4 St. Paul's Chapel
5 St. Peter's Church
6 Trinity Church

Civic Center Synagogue

49 White Street,
near Church Street
(212) 966-7141
www.civiccentersynagogue.org

Within a historic district

A flame is supposed to come to your mind when looking at the bulbous front of this 1969 synagogue by William N. Breger. But if you see a five-story, marble-clad pot-bellied stove instead, at least give credit to the Civic Center Synagogue, known formally as Congregation Shaare Zedek, for trying to find a distinct modernist vocabulary for an inner-city house of worship. There is an ethereal quality to the building, which seems to float overhead as you approach. In the sanctuary, where the bulbous wall is concave rather than convex, the play of light and shadow can be quite sublime.

Shaare Zedek (Gates of Justice) was founded in 1938 to serve textile workers and civil servants in the neighborhood. Today it also caters to the growing residential and artistic population of lower Manhattan, with a Hebrew School, an art gallery and a poetry reading series. "My firm belief is that traditional Judaism can be a vehicle for anyone's Jewish expression," says Jonathan Wilson Glass, who became rabbi in 1989.

In keeping with its tradition of giving working people a place to pray, each business day the synagogue offers the Minyan and Breakfast Club at 7:20 a.m., 7:30 on Friday. There are services at 12:40, 1:40 and 5:10 p.m., Monday through Thursday. Sabbath services are at 10 minutes after sundown on Friday and 9:30 a.m. Saturday.

John Street Church

44 John Street,
near Nassau Street
(212) 269-0014

Designated landmark

Ever since John and Charles Wesley's religious movement took root in American soil, this site has been the home of Methodist worship: in the Wesley Chapel of 1768, in an 1817 church and, since 1841, in the present structure—a touch of diminutive antebellum tranquillity among the canyons of the financial district. In recent years, the venerable church was safeguarded by the sale of its air rights to developers next door.

Organized by Philip Embury, an Irish preacher who immigrated to America in 1760, John Street is the oldest continuous Methodist congregation in North America. It is also, indirectly, the birthplace of the African Methodist Episcopal Zion Church, begun in 1796 by a group including Peter Williams, a tobacco merchant and former slave who had been sexton of the Wesley Chapel.

A bit of that old chapel still survives. It is said that its beams support the pulpit of the Park Avenue Methodist Church of 1927, at 106 East 86th Street. Historical relics from John Street may go back even further than Methodism. Human bones were found on the site in 1986. Because it was unclear whether they came from the old churchyard or an ancient native settlement, the Rev. Warren L. Danskin arranged for reburial in a Methodist-Mohawk ceremony.

Below the sanctuary is the Wesley Chapel Museum, containing memorabilia from early Methodist history, like the pulpit made by Embury in 1767, his signed Bible, a clock given by John Wesley in 1769 and an altar rail from 1785. Hours are noon to 4 p.m., Monday, Wednesday and Friday. Services are at 11 a.m. on Sunday and 12:15 p.m. on Wednesday.

Shrine of St. Elizabeth Ann Seton

7 and 8 State Street,
opposite Battery Park
(212) 269-6865
ourladyoftherosary.catholic.org

Designated landmark

At the southern tip of Manhattan, incomparably situated overlooking Battery Park, are the Church of Our Lady of the Rosary, built in 1964, and the adjoining James Watson house, begun in 1793, which is now the Shrine of St. Elizabeth Ann Seton, the first native-born American to be canonized. She lived on this site from 1801 to 1803 with her husband, William, and five children. In an effort to revive William's failing health, the couple sailed to Italy in 1803. He died in Pisa later that year but she stayed on to recover from her own maladies. Though Episcopalian, she became immersed in the Catholic faith while there. In 1804 she returned to New York and converted to Catholicism at St. Peter's Church on Barclay Street. She moved to Maryland in 1808, opened a school in Baltimore and organized the first American Catholic community for women, the Sisters of Charity of St. Joseph, in 1809. Known as the "mother of the American parochial school," she was canonized in 1975 by Pope Paul VI.

The Shrine of St. Elizabeth Ann Seton is open from the 7:05 a.m. Mass until 5:30 p.m., Monday through Friday. Other daily Masses are at 8:05 a.m., noon and 1:05 p.m. Sunday Masses are at 9 a.m. and noon; Saturday Mass is at noon.

St. Paul's Chapel

Broadway,
at Fulton Street
(212) 602-0800
www.trinitywallstreet.org

Designated landmark

From an ancient churchyard at Fulton Street rises a stone chapel, worthy of 18th-century London, that heard the fervent prayers of the men who created the new government of the United States on April 30, 1789.

Though it is hard now to imagine New York as the nation's capital, St. Paul's Chapel of Trinity parish was the scene of a thanksgiving service on that day, after George Washington was inaugurated president. The honor of conducting the service fell to St. Paul's—and not Trinity—because the mother church at Wall Street had burned in the great fire of 1776 and had not yet been rebuilt. Even after inauguration day, President Washington continued to worship at St. Paul's. He lived eight blocks south, at 39 Broadway, until the capital moved to Philadelphia in 1790.

Seemingly unchanged since the infancy of the republic, the chastely delicate architecture of Manhattan's oldest church practically invites you to listen for the sound of the founders' ghosts.

And the history of St. Paul's goes back further yet. Quite literally Colonial in style, it was constructed from 1764 to 1766, when New York was a British colony. London was the arbiter of style and St. Paul's seems to have been patterned after St. Martin-in-the-Fields, which had been rebuilt in 1724 by James Gibbs. Thomas McBean, a pupil of Gibbs, is frequently credited with the design of St. Paul's, although recent scholarship assigns an important role to Andrew Gautier.

St. Paul's was built to serve Trinity communicants who lived out in the countryside. Wheat fields surrounded it, and the Hudson River could be seen to the west. The Broadway porch, with St. Paul in the pediment, was added from 1767 to 1768; the noble wooden steeple, by James Crommelin Lawrence, in 1794. The "Glory" carving over the altar, showing Mount Sinai in clouds and lightning, was designed by Pierre L'Enfant, the architect who planned Washington, D.C. The chandeliers, added in 1802, are from Waterford, Ireland.

President Washington's pew is still set aside, and was occupied by President George Bush on a visit in 1989 to mark the bicentenary of the inauguration. But it is not only presidents who are welcomed here. Beginning in 1982, St. Paul's offered its balcony as a shelter for homeless men, whose cots and footlockers were arrayed around the mahogany organ case.

The Holy Eucharist service is on Sunday at 8 a.m. There is a concert at noon on Monday.

St. Peter's Church

Pierre Toussaint Square
22 Barclay Street,
at Church Street
(212) 233-8355

Designated landmark

This somber temple exudes antiquity, nobly bearing the mantle of three centuries of Catholic history. As Cardinal Terence J. Cooke said, "It all began here." Established in 1785, St. Peter's was the first Catholic parish in the state, and its members have always worshiped on this site.

In the 1780s, Masses were celebrated in a loft over a carpenter's shop on Barclay Street. Leading the move for a proper church was the French consul, Hector St. John de Crèvecoeur, who petitioned the city in 1785 for a place where Catholics could build a "decent edifice to adore God there according to their consciences." Trinity Corporation made five lots available at Barclay and Church Streets. The cornerstone of St. Peter's was laid by Don Diego de Gardoqui, the minister of Spain. The church opened in 1786 and the first parish school was established here in 1800.

Within 50 years, the old church was literally falling apart. The present church, built from 1836 to 1840 and supported by six gigantic granite Ionic columns, looks as if it could stand for several millennia. The design was once attributed to Isaiah Rogers, but is now more commonly assigned to John R. Haggerty and Thomas Thomas.

St. Peter's began midday services in 1906 for workers in the area. Mission churches to the Syrian population of lower Manhattan were established in the early 20th century: St. Joseph's Maronite Church stood on Washington Street until the construction of the Brooklyn-Battery Tunnel in the 1940s. To serve the growing number of new residents downtown, St. Peter's opened the small St. Joseph's Chapel at Battery Park City in 1983.

Being in the financial district, St. Peter's offers six Masses each weekday, twice as many as on Sunday. On holy days, the number goes up to 20 Masses, plus 12 more at St. Joseph's Chapel.

Trinity Church

Broadway,
at Wall Street
(212) 602-0800
www.trinitywallstreet.org

Designated landmark

King William III was the sovereign of New York City when its Anglican citizens first worshiped in a barnlike church on "the Broad Way," near the wall that marked the northern end of town. More than 300 years later, Trinity Church remains on the same spot. Its continuity alone gives it legendary status, as does its symbolic role as a spiritual counterpoint to Mammon, embodied by the nearby financial houses of Wall Street.

A charter from King William was granted on May 6, 1697. It called for Trinity parish to pay an annual rent of one peppercorn to the crown. While history does not record how faithfully that was discharged over time, Trinity covered its bases in 1976 by handing over 279 peppercorns—one for each year—to Queen Elizabeth II during her visit to the church.

The first Trinity was built in 1698 in a municipal cemetery. In fact, the oldest grave here, that of a boy named Richard Churcher, antedates Trinity by 15 years. Other burials and memorials include Alexander Hamilton; Robert Fulton; William Bradford, who published New York's first newspaper; and Captain James Lawrence, who didn't give up the ship. (The parish graveyard was moved in 1843 to upper Manhattan, between 153rd and 155th Streets, and now surrounds the Church of the Intercession.)

Trinity's destiny as an extraordinarily rich and powerful institution was cast by Queen Anne in 1705, when she enlarged the church's holdings to 215 acres, a parcel stretching along the Hudson from Fulton to Christopher Street. They called it the Queen's Farm. We call it Tribeca and the West Village.

As the city grew, Trinity's communicants dispersed and opened chapels wherever they settled. Long before a cathedral was envisioned, Trinity served as the mother church of a great ecclesiastical network. The first chapel, St. George's, opened in 1752 and evolved into the present church on Stuyvesant Square. Intercession, St. Augustine's, St. Luke's and even what is now St. Sava Serbian Orthodox Cathedral were all Trinity chapels at one time. The most venerable is surely St. Paul's, which alone remains a Trinity subsidiary.

The second Trinity Church, attributed to James Robinson or Josiah Brady, was consecrated in 1790 and lasted until a heavy snowfall in 1839 compelled its demolition.

Richard Upjohn designed the present building, which was consecrated in 1846 and influenced perhaps by Augustus Pugin's Church of St. Giles, in Cheadle, Staffordshire. The prolific and influential Upjohn also designed Trinity Chapel (now St. Sava), the Church of the Ascension and the Church of the Holy Communion (now Limelight).

Astonishing in many ways, Trinity Church was, first of all, the tallest building in New York and remained so for four decades. Its 280-foot, 5-inch spire is equal to a 24-story office tower. Trinity was topped by a controversial cross and, unlike most of its contemporaries, it made great use of stained glass.

The Chapel of All Saints, by Thomas Nash, was added in 1913; the Bishop William T. Manning Memorial Wing, by Adams & Woodbridge, in 1966. Manning succeeded Trinity's best-known rector, the Rev. Morgan Dix, who served from 1862 to 1908, during which time Trinity fended off claimants to its acreage, as well as the popular perception that it was no better than a slumlord. Though it long ago shed its tenement properties, Trinity remains a large commercial landlord, with more than

two dozen buildings, many of them along Hudson Street.

A 1990 façade restoration revealed statuary and other architectural details that had been obscured since the church was covered with coatings to protect it from pollution in the 1920s and late 50s. But the price for seeing clean, crisp, chocolate-brown sandstone was an undeniable loss of the gravitas that had adhered to the walls along with the soot.

In addition to being one of the most historic churches in New York, Trinity is one of the most active. There are two Holy Eucharist services on Sunday at 9 and 11:15 a.m. Holy Eucharist and morning prayer services are offered Monday through Saturday, with evening prayers daily. Tours are given every day at 2 p.m. and after the 11:15 service on Sunday. The museum is open daily from 9 to 11:45 a.m. and 1 to 3:45 p.m.; Saturday, 10 a.m. to 3:45 p.m.; Sunday, 1 to 3:45 p.m. A concert is held every Thursday at 1 p.m. There is a bookstore and gift shop. Among its many cultural, social-service and spiritual programs, Trinity has a welcome center for visitors from 10 a.m. to noon and 1 to 2:30 p.m., Sunday through Friday.

Another notable house of worship in the area:

Seamen's Church Institute
241 Water Street, near Peck Slip
Within a historic district

Once a floating chapel for sailors, the Institute moved in 1991 to this building by James Stewart Polshek & Partners. The design of the chapel is exceptionally cool and tranquil.

Chinatown, Little Italy and the Lower East Side

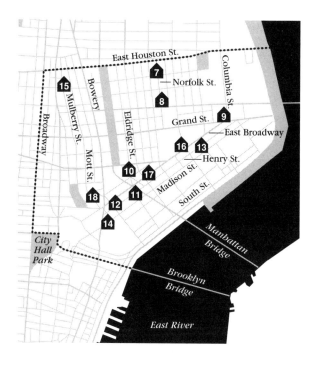

7 Angel Orensanz Foundation

8 Congregation Beth Hamedrash Hagodol

9 Bialystoker Synagogue

10 Eldridge Street Synagogue

11 First Chinese Presbyterian Church

12 Mariners' Temple Baptist Church

13 St. Augustine's Church

14 St. James Church

15 St. Patrick's Old Cathedral

16 Shtiebl Row

17 Sung Tak Buddhist Association

18 Church of the Transfiguration

Angel Orensanz Foundation

172 Norfolk Street,
near Houston Street
(212) 529-7194
www.orensanz.org

Designated landmark

Gothic architecture makes for espe-cially haunting ruins. And that is just what this historic structure—actually the oldest existing synagogue building in New York City—had become by the early 1980s. Gothic architecture also poses a puzzle: why would a place of Jewish worship be designed in that most Christian of styles? One inference is that Congregation Anshe Chesed (People of Mercy), which built the synagogue in 1850, did not want to stand out too  much. So it cloaked its building in assimilationist garb, commissioning a design from Alexander Saeltzer that would be almost indistinguishable from a church, even though it was New York's largest synagogue at the time of its construction, with room for 700 men on the main floor and 500 women in the gallery.

Anshe Chesed, composed primarily of German Jews, was the forerunner of a congregation known as Beth El, which later merged into the prominent Temple Emanu-El. After Anshe Chesed moved away from Norfolk Street in 1874, this synagogue was used in turn by three other congregations, until it was abandoned in 1974.

The Spanish sculptor Angel Orensanz and his brother, Al, bought the ruined building in 1986 for use as a studio and artists' colony. In 1992 the Angel Orensanz Foundation Center for the Arts was established. The building is now the setting of art exhibits, concerts, performances such as Mandy Patinkin's *Mamaloshen*, and other events, like the wedding of Sarah Jessica Parker and Matthew Broderick.

The Gothic sanctuary, with its vaulted blue ceilings, pointed arches and ribbed vaults, is still in a state of poignant decrepitude.

Anyone wishing to visit the building can drop by or call in advance (to be sure it's open). Contact the Lower East Side Conservancy, (212) 598-1200 or www.nycjewishtours.com, which offers tours of this and other synagogues. There is a Reform Sabbath service on Friday evening.

Congregation Beth Hamedrash Hagodol

60 Norfolk Street, near Delancey Street (212) 674-3330

Designated landmark

The stout twin towers of this Gothic Revival landmark are a proud assertion of history in the face of the leveling forces of redevelopment. Built in 1850, the same year as Congregation Anshe Chesed four blocks to the north, this was originally the Norfolk Street Baptist Church, forerunner of the Riverside Church. The sanctuary was purchased in 1885 by Congregation Beth Hamedrash Hagodol (Great House of Study), an Orthodox Russian group founded by Rabbi Abraham Joseph Ash in 1852.

For five decades, the congregation has been led by Rabbi Ephraim Oshry of Kovno, Lithuania, who was instrumental in preserving historical artifacts of the Kovno ghetto during World War II. In 1967, when Beth Hamedrash Hagodol was threatened by urban renewal, Oshry secured a designation from the Landmarks Preservation Commission, thus preserving history for a second time.

Tours of Beth Hamedrash Hagodol are conducted by the Lower East Side Conservancy; call (212) 598-1200 or visit www.nycjewishtours.com.

Bialystoker Synagogue

7 Bialystoker Place (Willett Street),
near Grand Street
(212) 475-0165

Designated landmark

Plain enough on the outside, befitting its origins in 1826 as the Willett Street Methodist Church, this gable-roofed stone sanctuary was lavishly remodeled as a synagogue inside, with a richly carved two-story Ark, glittering stained-glass windows worthy of a jewel box and enormous chandeliers. It is the oldest building used as a synagogue in New York. (That distinguishes it from the oldest building constructed as a synagogue, the Angel Orensanz Foundation.)

Congregation Beth Haknesseth Anshe Bialystok (Synagogue of the People of Bialystok), founded in 1878, takes its name from the province and city of Bialystok, in northeastern Poland, once a hub of Jewish life in the Pale of Settlement—and, of course, the birthplace of the bialy. It acquired the Methodist church in 1905. While numerous synagogues around it were abandoned in the 1970s and 1980s, Bialystoker endured. In the 1990s it undertook a restoration of the sanctuary, including the stained glass.

The sign in front of Bialystoker says that it is open 365 days a year. In addition to Sabbath services on Friday evening and Saturday, there are four morning services daily, plus two more in the afternoon and another in the evening.

Eldridge Street Synagogue

12 Eldridge Street,
near Division Street
(212) 978-8800
www.eldridgestreet.org

Designated landmark

Extraordinary both for its architecture and its historical place as the first great house of worship built by eastern European Jews in America, the Eldridge Street Synagogue today is a poignant mix of ruin and revival as a decades-long restoration effort plays out while the small remaining congregation continues an unbroken line of worship going back to 1887, when the building was completed.

The congregation was founded in 1852 by Russian Jews and took the name K'hal Adath Jeshurun (Community of the Congregation of Israel). It later merged with
Anshe Lubz (People of Lubz, Poland). Membership swelled in the 1880s, thanks to the immigration from Eastern Europe, and the congregation commissioned Peter and Francis Herter to design a synagogue with a façade containing Gothic, Moorish and Romanesque elements symbolizing, through their shape and number, Jewish beliefs, holidays and history. The sanctuary has a 70-foot-high vaulted ceiling, stained-glass windows, brass fixtures and stenciled walls. The Ark is made of hand-carved walnut.

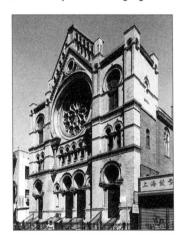

For almost half a century, thousands of worshipers attended, including such well-known actors as Sam Jaffe, Paul Muni and Edward G. Robinson; Dr. Jonas Salk, whose polio vaccine bears his name; and the artist Ben Shahn. On High Holy Days, the police had to be called in to control the crowds. But beginning in the 1920s, as immigration slowed and congregants moved away, the main sanctuary was used less often. It closed in the 1950s. Then as now, the small congregation used a lower-level room for services.

The building deteriorated. Everything from the foundation to the roof needed replacement or repair. First to the rescue was Gerard Wolfe, who organized Friends of the Eldridge Street Synagogue in the late 1970s. That was succeeded by the Eldridge Street Project, founded in 1986 by Roberta Brandes Gratz. It has raised and spent $6 million on restoration, stabilization and educational and cultural programs. It hopes to raise an additional $8 million to complete the restoration, designed by a team of preservation architects that includes Jill Gotthelf and Diane Kaese, with Richard Blinder.

Orthodox services are conducted at sundown on Friday and at 10 a.m. Saturday. Tours are conducted Sunday between 11 a.m. and 4 p.m., Tuesday and Thursday at 11:30 a.m. and 2:30 p.m., or by appointment. Reservations are required for groups of 10 or more. Admission is $4 for adults and $2.50 for students and the elderly. Concerts, lectures, exhibits, walking tours, workshops and cooking classes—including rugelach-baking lessons—are also offered.

First Chinese Presbyterian Church

61 Henry Street,
at Market Street
(212) 964-5488
www.fcpc.org

Designated landmark

Country-style churches can be found throughout Chinatown and the Lower East Side, gentle reminders of the rural past. Indeed, long before this sanctuary was occupied by Chinese Presbyterians, it was known as the "Kirk on Rutgers Farm," as it stands on land donated by Colonel Henry Rutgers, the benefactor of the State University of New Jersey and Rutgers Presbyterian Church. Built as the Northeast Dutch Reformed Church from 1817 to 1819, the sanctuary straddles the era between Georgian and Gothic architecture, with pointed-arch windows, under a simple gabled roof. The 1824 Henry Erben organ, though no longer in use, is still proudly on display, a link to the church's long past.

The building was transferred in 1866 to the New York Presbytery and renamed the Church of the Sea and Land, ministering to seamen. As Chinese workers moved to New York in the 1870s and 1880s, a new kind of inner-city ministry was born. The Rev. Huie Kin began a mission in 1885 on University Place that evolved into the First Chinese Presbyterian Church, of which he was pastor.

In 1951, the Chinese congregation moved into this church, which it shared with Sea and Land until 1972, when Manhattan's dwindling role as a seaport forced the closing of the mariners' group.

Sunday services are in Cantonese at 11 a.m. and in English at 1 p.m.

Mariners' Temple Baptist Church

3 Henry Street,
at Oliver Street
(212) 233-0423

Designated landmark

Rough-and-tumble New York was the surprising setting for several Greek Revival gems from America's early and brief Arcadian spell. This one was built from 1842 to 1844 and is attributed to Minard Lafever, architect of the Church of the Holy Apostles in Chelsea and the Church of St. Ann and the Holy Trinity in Brooklyn Heights. (Lafever may or may not have also had a hand in St. James Church nearby, which shares the distinctive type of façade known as distyle in antis: two columns framed by two pilasters.) Mariners' Temple, founded in 1795 to minister to seamen, was down to 60 members by 1983. But the Rev. Suzan D. Johnson Cook, the first African-American woman elected senior pastor of any American Baptist congregation, reinvigorated the place with the Hour of Power lunchtime service on Wednesdays and the Multi-Ethnic Learning Center.

The Sunday service is at 10 a.m. On Wednesday the Hour of Power is at noon, and Bible study is at 6 p.m. There is a prayer service on Thursday at noon.

St. Augustine's Church

290 Henry Street,
near Montgomery Street
(212) 673-5300

Designated landmark

It would be a mistake to pass by this appealingly simple stone church without going inside and climbing up to the attic. For St. Augustine's claim on the civic conscience rests in a feature that is all but hidden from view: two crude galleries on either side of the organ loft; a world away from the pews, tucked under the eaves, reached by a narrow staircase, with seating on shallow risers. According to civic and church lore, this was where slaves worshiped. Indeed, the sign-board at St. Augustine's declares it to be the "Home of New York City's Only Existing Slave Gallery." But is it? The church, originally known as All Saints, was consecrated in June 1828—11 months after emancipation took effect in New York State.

In a way, the chronology doesn't matter. The people made to worship in these galleries must have experienced a vast, immutable gulf separating them from the gentry below. And it is enormously moving to get a visceral, three-dimensional sense of how rigidly society was stratified and segregated, even in a house of the Lord.

Built by clipper-ship owners and presumably designed by John Heath, the church got its central tower in 1871. All Saints' merged in 1945 with St. Augustine's Chapel, an outpost of Trinity from East Houston Street. In 1952 the Rev. C. Kilmer Myers became vicar, and he later chronicled his experience in this often violent and lawless neighborhood in *Light the Dark Streets*. "A parish not in tension is not, in our day, a Christian parish," he wrote.

After more than 30 years as a Trinity chapel, St. Augustine's was spun off in 1976 as an independent parish. In the 1990s, under the Rev. Errol A. Harvey, who was also chairman of the black caucus in the Episcopal diocese, the church began offering one of the first programs of AIDS counseling for convicts and addicts.

Sunday morning services are at 8, 9 (children's worship) and 10 (with choir). There is a noon service Monday through Friday.

St. James Church

32 St. James Street,
near Madison Street
(212) 233-0161

Designated landmark

The Greek Revival nobility of this exceptionally old Roman Catholic church, with its crisp lines and broad front pediment, has been no guarantee against hard times. But the classical architecture helps conjure the days in the 1880s when this was the "leading Catholic parish in New York, not excepting the cathedral itself," in the words of Alfred E. Smith, who served as an altar boy here. He went on to become a four-term governor of New York State and the first Roman Catholic candidate for the United States presidency in 1928.

Constructed from 1835 to 1837, St. James has so many sophisticated architectural elements—including rosettes and a scrolled lintel cornice over the granite door—that its design has often been attributed to Minard Lafever.

It is also distinguished as an early 19th-century sanctuary that is still being used by the parish that built it, although not without troubles. In 1983 the Buildings Department ordered the church closed because the roof was in danger of collapsing. For the next three years, services were held in the basement and in the school across the street, while money was raised for needed repairs.

St. James is on the same block as the first Shearith Israel cemetery, the oldest physical vestige of a house of worship in Manhattan.

Sunday Masses are in English at 8:30, 10 and 11:30 a.m. and in Spanish at 11 a.m. Other days, Masses are at 8 a.m. and 5:30 p.m. On Thursday the 5:30 p.m. service is in Spanish.

St. Patrick's Old Cathedral

260 Mulberry Street,
at Prince Street
(212) 226-8075
www.oldsaintpatricks.org

Designated landmark

Defense of faith has carried a life-or-death meaning around the walls of old St. Patrick's, which Catholic New Yorkers had to save from nativist mobs intent on destruction.

The cornerstone was laid in 1809 by the Rev. Anthony Kohlmann, an Alsatian Jesuit who had arrived in New York a year earlier to take charge of the struggling young diocese. Built on the site of the cemetery used by St. Peter's Church, the cathedral was dedicated to the apostle of Ireland and designed by Joseph François Mangin, one of the architects of City Hall.

A very early essay in Gothic Revival, St. Patrick's was, when finished in 1815, the largest religious structure in New York. It was here that St. John Neumann was ordained in 1836. King Louis Philippe of France donated stained-glass windows made in Sèvres, but they were the wrong size, so Archbishop John J. Hughes gave them to a seminary chapel in the Bronx that is now the Fordham University Church.

Violence between nativist agitators and Irish Catholics flared several times before a crowd gathered in 1836 to attack the cathedral. Warned in advance, defenders cut musket ports in the brick wall and stationed armed sentinels on Prince Street. As recounted in *Gotham,* a history of New York by Edwin G. Burrows and Mike Wallace, the mob retreated after learning from scouts of the "fearsomeness of the Gaels' military preparations and the fortress-like impregnability of their walled cathedral."

What the Know-nothings couldn't achieve, an accident accomplished in 1866. The cathedral burned down to the exterior stone walls. It was rebuilt to designs by Henry Engelbert and rededicated on St. Patrick's Day, 1868. (During this period, two St. Patrick's Cathedrals were being built at the same time.)

Hughes's successor, John McCloskey, was invested as the first American cardinal here in 1875. Only four years later, however, the new St. Patrick's opened and this sanctuary took the role of parish church for succeeding generations of Italians, Dominicans and Chinese. The remains of Pierre Toussaint were exhumed from the graveyard in 1990 as part of the investigation into his possible canonization as America's first black saint, and then moved to the crypt of the uptown cathedral.

Still set off beautifully behind the same high brick walls from the dense streets of what was once Little Italy, St. Patrick's has a surprisingly sumptuous interior that is well worth a visit. If you have a sense of déjà vu, it's because the christening scene from *The Godfather,* was filmed here.

The former cathedral is open every day but Wednesday, from 8 a.m. to 1 p.m. and from 3:30 p.m. until the completion of that day's services. Masses are said in English every day and in Spanish four days a week. The 7:30 p.m. Mass on Sunday is said to have "an Irish accent." One of the dozen or so 19th-century Henry Erben organs still surviving in New York City can be found—and heard—here.

Shtiebl Row

From hundreds of villages in eastern Europe, hundreds of thousands of Jews immigrated to the metropolis around the turn of the century and then promptly redrew their village boundaries around their own small congregations, known as chavarot. Too independent to be subsumed into larger synagogues and too poor to build their own, these chavarot used any empty space they could afford, including storefronts and tenements. The small rooms in which they worshiped were known as shtieblach. More than 500 were established, many of them on a stretch of East Broadway known as Shtiebl Row, the citadel of Orthodoxy. Today there are still 10 or 12 shtieblach on these two blocks. And the recent return of Orthodox families to the area seems to have revivified Shtiebl Row after decades of decline.

In the midst of the row is the Young Israel Synagogue, home of the oldest congregation in the worldwide Orthodox movement called Young Israel. It traces its origins to a 1911 lecture on Judaism by the famous Reform rabbi, Stephen S. Wise. A group of Orthodox youths in attendance were outraged when collection baskets were passed on the Sabbath. Looking for a way to resist assimilation while participating in American life, the young men turned to Rabbi Judah L. Magnes for counsel. He delivered a series of lectures in the Kalvarier Shul on Pike Street (now the Sung Tak Buddhist Association), leading to the establishment of the Young Israel movement in 1912. The name was suggested to Magnes when someone in the crowd shouted, "We in America are the young of Israel!"

The Young Israel congregation first worshiped in storefront space on Shtiebl Row. In 1929 it opened its present sanctuary at 235 East Broadway, a former tenement that had been occupied by the Hebrew Immigrant Aid Society.

Sabbath services at Young Israel, (212) 732-0966, begin at sundown on Friday and 8:45 a.m. and 4:25 p.m. on Saturday. To learn more about Shtiebl Row, contact the Lower East Side Conservancy, (212) 598-1200 or www.nyjewishtours.com.

Sung Tak Buddhist Association

13 Pike Street,
near East Broadway
(212) 587-5936

Designated landmark

This handsome four-story structure is a kind of architectural metaphor for the Lower East Side: built to serve a vital Jewish community, transmogrified into an abandoned eyesore and then revived—though much modified—in Chinese hands.

Immigrants from the village of Kalwarie on the Polish-Lithuanian border joined in 1899 with members of Congregation Beth Hamedrash Livne Yisroel Yelide Polen to form Congregation B'nai Israel Kalwarie (Sons of Israel). They built this synagogue, designed by Alfred E. Badt, from 1903 to 1904. Known as the Kalvarier Shul or Pike Street Shul, its façade is dominated by tall, slender Romanesque arched windows, recalling the synagogues of Shaaray Tefila, 160 West 82nd Street, and Kehilath Jeshurun, 117 East 85th Street. The dwindling congregation remained until the 1970s.

Even as the Jewish population declined, the number of Chinese New Yorkers was growing rapidly. With tens of thousands of new arrivals, Chinatown pushed well beyond its traditional borders into

the surrounding Italian and Jewish quarters, a transformation clearly illustrated in 1994, when the derelict Kalvarier Shul was sold and converted into a Buddhist temple.

The temple is open every day from 9 a.m. until 6 p.m. and will feed anyone over 60 years old free of charge. Services in Cantonese are held at 10:30 a.m. on Sunday and on the first and fifteenth of the month.

44

Church of the Transfiguration

Transfiguration, indeed. Bought by the Roman church from the Anglicans for a parish founded by a Cuban priest to serve an Irish and then Italian population, it evolved over time into a center of the Chinese community, with a school where most of the children are Buddhist.

The story begins in 1801 with the building of Zion English Lutheran Church, later Zion Episcopal. It was bought in 1853 by Transfiguration, known as the Church of the Immigrants. This Catholic parish was founded in 1827 by the Rev. Felix Varela y Morales, little known today by New Yorkers but revered in his native Cuba as a candidate for sainthood. An advocate of independence from Spain (which is why he was exiled here), Varela was a social reformer, philosopher, the vicar general of the archdiocese and publisher of an early Spanish-language newspaper, *El Habañero* (The Havanan). Paying homage, Pope John Paul II said Varela was the "best synthesis" of Christian faith and Cuban culture.

Transfiguration added its steeple, by Henry Engelbert, in 1868. Italians, including a young Jimmy Durante, followed the Irish in the parish. Under the Salesians and Maryknoll Fathers, the church started ministering to Chinese residents. Cantonese sermons began in the 1950s, and in 1976 the Rev. Mark Cheung became the first Chinese pastor. Transfiguration School, founded by Varela in 1832, was opened to all faiths in 1969.

Sunday Mass is said in Mandarin at 9 a.m., Cantonese at 11:30 and English at 10:15 a.m., 12:45 and 6 p.m. From Monday through Saturday, the Cantonese Mass is at 8 a.m., the English at 12:10 p.m.

Greenwich Village and the East Village

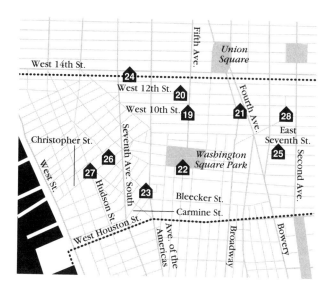

19 Church of the Ascension
20 First Presbyterian Church
21 Grace Church
22 Judson Memorial Church
23 Church of Our Lady of Pompei
24 Portico Place Apartments

25 St. George Ukrainian Catholic Church
26 St. John Lutheran
27 Church of St. Luke in the Fields
28 St. Mark's Church in-the-Bowery

Church of the Ascension

Not long after opening on Fifth Avenue, the Church of the Ascension drew the President of the United States, John Tyler, for his wedding in June 1844 to the very much younger Julia Gardiner, of the Gardiners Island family. The couple left the church the "laughing-stock of this city," John Quincy Adams said.

Ascension survived with its dignity intact, however. Founded in 1827 on Canal Street, the Episcopal parish moved to the newly fashionable Fifth Avenue in 1841. Its sanctuary was designed by Richard Upjohn, who was known to favor High Church features like deep chancels. The Rev. Manton Eastburn, of the more evangelical Low Church school of Episcopalianism, blocked any such possibility by purchasing the parcel directly behind the church for a rectory. In the 1880s the chancel was magnificently adorned by Stanford White and John La Farge, whose 30-by-35-foot mural depicting the ascension of Christ into heaven is the greatest artistic treasure in the church. There is also stained glass by La Farge, D. Maitland Armstrong and the Tiffany Glass Company.

Just after the stock market crash of 1929, the Rev. Donald Bradshaw Aldrich opened the doors of the Fifth Avenue sanctuary around the clock, every day of the year, as a place of prayer and meditation. By the 1960s, it was estimated that some 30,000 visitors a year availed themselves of the Church of the Open Door, whose illuminated altar was visible to passersby. Ascension is no longer open all day but it still welcomes the public with everything from a highly regarded musical program to a food pantry.

Ascension opens its gates to the garden and doors to the sanctuary every day from noon to 2 p.m., and at 5 p.m. in preparation for the 6 p.m. service. On Sunday there are services at 9 and 11 a.m. Tours for groups wishing to take a closer look at the artwork and stained glass can be arranged, but they must be their own guides. The Voices of Ascension, an outstanding professional choir, uses the church for its concerts. For more information, call (212) 254-8553

First Presbyterian Church

12 West 12th Street,
at Fifth Avenue
(212) 675-6150
www.firstpresnyc.org

Within a historic district

You're in Greenwich Village but Trinity Church comes to mind: an early Gothic Revival tower rises proudly from an improbably expansive churchyard, framed by high-rises, overlooking a vital thoroughfare. The similarities between Old Trinity and Old First don't end there. First Presbyterian also began on Wall Street—not too many years after Trinity—in 1716. And it was the mother church in an early ecclesiastical hub-and-spoke system that yielded significant congregations in their own right: Brick Church in 1767, Rutgers Church in 1798 and the Cedar Street Church (now Fifth Avenue Presbyterian) in 1808.

Unlike Trinity, however, First Presbyterian moved uptown when it became clear that lower Manhattan would be given over almost entirely to business. It built its present church from 1845 to 1846 on a blockfront between 11th and 12th Streets. The verdant grounds, ringed by a cast-iron fence, are an extraordinary sight today. Designed by Joseph C. Wells, the building was patterned on the Church of St. Saviour in Bath, England, with a tower modeled on that of Magdalen College, Oxford. The south transept, by McKim, Mead & White, was added in 1893.

Old First merged in 1918 with the Rev. Charles H. Parkhurst's Madison Square church and the University Place congregation. Before moving uptown to Riverside Church, the Rev. Harry Emerson Fosdick was assistant pastor here, causing a storm of controversy in 1922—

three years before the Scopes Trial—when he asserted that Darwinism was not inconsistent with the Christian faith.

A church house was added in 1960. The architect, Edgar Tafel, blended Gothic details with the Prairie style of Frank Lloyd Wright, under whom Tafel studied.

Inside the old church is a lovely suite of stained-glass windows by Tiffany, David Maitland Armstrong, Charles Lamb and Frank Lathrop. Those on the north side depict Scriptural scenes; those on the south highlight the history of Protestantism. The windows were restored under the supervision of the noted conservator William Stivale and rededicated in 1988. "Their major function," said the co-pastor, the Rev. John Brown Macnab, "is to demonstrate that we are part of an ongoing pilgrimage."

Sunday services are at 11 a.m.; noonday prayers on Monday and Wednesday at 12:15 p.m. The church is open for meditation on Friday from 12:15 to 12:45 p.m.

Grace Church

800 Broadway,
at East 10th Street
(212) 254-2000
www.gracenyc.org

Designated landmark

A bend in Broadway gives Grace Church a special spot in the cityscape, allowing its marble Gothic spire to be seen from as far away as City Hall Park; "a pinnacle of alabaster," as the civic chronicler George Templeton Strong wrote in 1870, or, on a wintry twilight, a "great crystal of rose quartz."

Legend ascribes the bend to Henry Brevoort, who resisted efforts to straighten the road at the expense of his apple orchard. Happily for posterity, the young architect James Renwick Jr. (a Brevoort on his mother's side) knew how to handle so special a site, bestowing on it a slender tower that seems to float over Broadway. Grace was completed in 1846. Seven years later, Renwick was approached to design St. Patrick's Cathedral.

Set in a wall of Grace Church is the 1806 foundation stone from the first sanctuary, which stood at Broadway and Rector Street. The 10th Street complex grew by accretion. Renwick's rectory, a Gothic Revival mansion on Broadway, was added in 1847. The Chantry was built in 1879 and Grace House in 1881. Stained-glass windows by Clayton & Bell and Henry Holiday arrived in the late 19th century. On Fourth Avenue are the charming Gothic buildings of the Grace Church School, built from 1881 to 1907. A mission chapel was built on East 14th Street that is now the Roman Catholic Church of the Immaculate Conception.

In the 19th century, Grace was the church for high society, of which the sexton here, Isaac Hull Brown, was supreme arbiter. "To be

married or buried within its walls has been ever considered the height of felicity," it was said. But the wedding in 1863 of two little people, Lavinia Warren and Charles S. Stratton (better known as General Tom Thumb), was protested by parishioners who thought it a spectacle. It was left to the Rev. Thomas House Taylor to defend the ceremony by quoting Stratton: "It is true we are little, but we are as God made us, perfect in our littleness!"

Taylor was followed as rector by the Rev. Henry Codman Potter, who later initiated the Cathedral of St. John the Divine as Bishop of New York.

A 1974 plan to replace the school buildings with a new gym met considerable opposition, and the design was changed to spare the historic façades. In the main church, a restoration of the stained-glass windows, by Cummings Studio of North Adams, Mass., was completed in 2000.

It would probably startle Sexton Brown to know that his church now prides itself in operating a year-round shelter for six homeless "guests." But it might not surprise Tom Thumb.

Morning prayer is at 11 on Sunday, with Holy Communion on the first Sunday of the month. Holy Eucharist services are on Sunday, 9 a.m. and 6 p.m.; Wednesday, 6 p.m. Morning prayer at 7:30, Monday through Friday; 9 on Saturday. Evening prayer at 6 on Monday, Tuesday, Thursday and Friday. Special services for children on Sunday at 11 a.m. Musical programs include the Choir of Men and Boys, St. Cecilia Chorus for girls, an adult choir and the Grace Church Choral Society. Tours can be arranged by calling the parish office. A handsome guidebook is available in the office for $5.

Judson Memorial Church

55 Washington Square South,
at Thompson Street
(212) 477-0351
www.judson.org

Designated landmark

If the Washington Arch is the gateway to Greenwich Village, the 10-tiered, golden-brick tower of Judson Memorial Church on the other side of Washington Square is the triumphal column, proclaiming an institution that could have only evolved in the Village, with its marvelous jumble of religious, social, political and cultural missions.

It was, at its origin, associated with the Judson family. The Rev. Edward Judson was called in 1881 to the Berean Baptist Church. He expanded it so significantly that new quarters were needed. The present church, by Stanford White of McKim, Mead & White, was built from 1890 to 1893 and dedicated to Judson's father, Adoniram, a famous missionary. Edward's dream was to serve both gentry and immigrants. "If the rich and poor are ever to meet together," he said, "it must be in the poor man's territory." The church was open all week, offering health care, employment guidance, sewing classes, even firewood and fresh milk. In the 1950s and '60s the church opened itself to dancers, poets, performers and artists like Jim Dine, Claes Oldenburg and Red Grooms.

Under the Rev. Peter Laarman in the 1990s, the church continued to see itself on the side of self-empowerment, but it also took care of its physical plant. Stained-glass windows by John La Farge, installed between 1892 and 1915, were restored by the Cummings Studio. The results were breathtaking. When the sun hits, certain colors leap to the foreground like French horns slicing through the sound of a symphony orchestra. At one moment, it is the gold on the edge of the Scriptures held by St. Anthony; at another, it is the scarlet in the legs of St. George, whose limbs are rendered as intricately as in an anatomical diagram. A counterpoint to the dazzle is the grape-and-violet robe of St. Peter, so lush in the layering of purples that it looks as if it had been cut from velour rather than glass.

Judson, which is affiliated with both the American Baptist Churches and the United Church of Christ, continues to take pride in its dedication to the arts and to human rights. It sponsors art shows and holds an open discussion of topical events every Sunday before the 11 a.m. service. It is open to visitors on Wednesday from noon until 4 p.m.

Church of Our Lady of Pompei

25 Carmine Street,
at Bleecker Street
(212) 989-6805

Although the Italian Greenwich Village is largely a memory, its cynosure—a limestone, copper-domed steeple as slender as a ceremonial giglio tower—still serves as an exuberant marker of this long-vital community.

In 1892 the Rev. Pietro Bandini of the Scalabrinian missionary society opened a chapel to Our Lady of Pompei on Waverly Place. The chapel moved to Sullivan Street and became a parish, with Luigi Vittorio Fugazy, grandfather of the businessman William D. Fugazy, among its trustees. It moved in 1898 to a Greek Revival church on Bleecker Street that had been used by St. Benedict the Moor parish. Mother Frances Xavier Cabrini, the first American saint, briefly taught at Pompei during this time.

The Rev. Antonio Demo, a Scalabrinian, became pastor in 1900. For the next 35 years, he was an important figure in the Village, especially in the wake of the Triangle Shirtwaist fire of 1911, which killed at least 18 of his parishioners. He was responsible for building the present church, from 1926 to 1928, after New York announced that it would extend Sixth Avenue southward through the old property. For the new site, Matthew Del Gaudio designed a combination church, school, convent and rectory. In 1941, five years after Demo's death, a nearby square was renamed in his honor.

In recent years, Our Lady of Pompei parish has included sizable numbers of Vietnamese and Filipino members.

Except for the 11 a.m. Mass in Italian on Sunday, all services are in English. There is a Saturday vigil at 5 p.m., followed by services at 9 a.m., 12:15 p.m. and 6 p.m. Weekday services are at 7 and 8:30 a.m. and 12:05 p.m.

Portico Place Apartments

With a stately, sheltering portico that seems almost to embrace the whole block, the Thirteenth Street Presbyterian Church opened in 1847. Attributed to Samuel Thomson, it was based on the Theseion in Athens, which was begun in 449 B.C. and had itself been converted into a church.

From 1954 to 1974, the 13th Street sanctuary was the home of both the Village Presbyterian Church, under the Rev. Jesse W. Stitt, and the Brotherhood Synagogue, founded by Rabbi Irving J. Block. This celebrated ecumenical arrangement began to fray in the early 1970s and dissolved completely during the Arab-Israeli war of 1973. Rabbi Block posted a notice on the outdoor bulletin board: "May there be victory and peace for Israel." The pastor, the Rev. William Glenesk, promptly apologized in his church bulletin to "our friends, Arab, non-Zionist Jews and all who are offended by the arrogant, self-righteous sign." Rabbi Block regarded this as a "declaration of war against the Jewish people." The synagogue moved out. The church closed in 1975.

Seven years later, the building was converted into a small co-op. To preserve the dignity of this noble temple front, the architect, Stephen B. Jacobs, moved the new residential entrance to the side. A beguiling touch is the signboard for "The Village Presbyterian Church" out front, posted with what look like hymn numbers: 141, 143, 145. These are in fact the street addresses.

St. George Ukrainian Catholic Church

30 East Seventh Street,
at Taras Shevchenko Place
(212) 674-1615
www.brama.com/stgeorge

While many other ethnic enclaves in Manhattan were vanishing in the latter half of the 20th century, the Catholics of Little Ukraine built this domed Byzantine Contemporary church, firmly rooted on the spot where they had worshiped for more than six decades. The parish was founded in 1905 on East 20th Street and moved in 1911 to the old Seventh Street Methodist Church on this site, just across the street from McSorley's legendary saloon. The present church was built from 1976 to 1978 and was designed by Apollinaire Osadca. Its façade includes mosaic panels showing St. George Cathedral in Lviv and St. Sophia Cathedral in Kiev. At the end of the 1990s the church estimated that about 25,000 Ukrainians still lived in this area.

All the divine liturgies at St. George are in Ukrainian. On Sunday, they are said at 7:30, 9 and 10 a.m., noon and 4 p.m; Monday through Saturday at 6:30, 8 and 8:30 a.m., and Saturday evenings at 6. The rosary is recited at 8:30 on Sunday and 7:30 on other days.

St. John Lutheran Church

81 Christopher Street,
near Bleecker Street
(212) 242-5737

Within a historic district

Hiding in plain sight on a raucous Greenwich Village thorough-fare is one of the oldest houses of worship in Manhattan, built from 1821 to 1822 as the Eighth Presbyterian Church. You might be fooled at first by some of the Victorian gewgaws added in an 1886 alteration by Berg & Clark, but the essential form is a barnlike, gabled Georgian structure. The Presbyterians gave up the church in 1842 to St. Matthew's Episcopal, which was here until 1858, when the building was turned over to the German Lutherans. (Note the old sign in the pediment: "Deutsche Evangelisch-Lutherische St. Johannes Kirche.") At the time, German immigrants constituted roughly one-quarter of the entire population of New York City. While their principal settle-ment was east of the Bowery, there was a flourishing German community in Greenwich Village that all but disappeared after World War I.

In the 1990s audiences came here for *Tony 'n' Tina's Wedding,* an off-Broadway production in which theater-goers mingled with the cast as if they were attending an actual ceremony.

Services at St. John's are at 11 a.m. on Sunday and holy days. Visits can be arranged by calling the office between noon and 3 p.m.

Church of St. Luke in the Fields

487 Hudson Street,
near Christopher Street
(212) 924-0562
www.stlukeinthefields.org

Within a historic district

North of New York City in the early 19th century, the pleasant country village of Greenwich served as a haven from the summertime pestilence of yellow fever. In honor of Luke, the physician evangelist, Episcopal villagers organized a church in 1820. Clement Clarke Moore, best remembered for the poem "A Visit from St. Nicholas," drew up a plan, but the building contract was given to John Heath. Both have been credited with this church, which was constructed from 1821 to 1822.

After a fire at the church in 1886, the St. Luke congregation built a new church at Convent Avenue and West 141st Street, designed by R. H. Robertson. It opened in 1892 and continues to this day, meaning that—yes—there are two Episcopal St. Lukes in Manhattan.

The Hudson Street sanctuary became a mission chapel of Trinity parish in 1892. A gym was added to the complex in 1927; a garden, playground and school completed the complex in 1951. St. Luke's Chapel became an independent parish in 1976. Three years later, it was one of the first churches in the Anglican Communion to appoint a woman, Lucia P. Ballantine, as associate rector.

Fire struck again in March 1981, gutting the building ruinously. Even as firefighters were extinguishing the blaze, however, onlookers were already pledging money for reconstruction. One young girl raised hundreds of dollars playing her violin on the sidewalk outside the church. The Rev. Ledlie I. Laughlin Jr. led services in the gym as reconstruction proceeded, to designs by Hardy Holzman Pfeiffer Associates. St. Luke's was reconsecrated in 1985.

With its embrace of gay Villagers, the parish was also hard hit by AIDS. Fittingly, its lovely, chaste sanctuary was the setting of a memorial service scene in the 1990 movie, *Longtime Companion*.

There are three services on Sunday, evening services every weekday and morning services on Tuesday and Thursday. A professional choir sings at the 11:15 Sunday service, sometimes joined by musicians or a full orchestra. Boy and girl choristers sing at the 9:15 service. In addition, the West Village Chorale gives two concerts here each year. The lush garden, with its winding, narrow paths, is a neighborhood oasis.

St. Mark's Church in-the-Bowery

131 East 10th Street,
at Stuyvesant Street
(212) 674-6377
www.saintmarkschurch.org

Designated landmark

I don't know if the East Village is 'way out' because of St. Mark's or if St. Mark's is 'way out' because of the East Village," said Bishop Paul Moore Jr. of the Episcopal diocese in 1986. "But certainly the church and the neighborhood share a free spirit."

Maybe it's in the soil. It was to this farm, or bouwerie, that Governor Peter Stuyvesant retired after Nieuw Amsterdam was surrendered to the British. The diagonal route of Stuyvesant Street marks the path of a farm road on which Stuyvesant built a chapel in 1660. He was buried here— and his remains remain. In 1793 Stuyvesant's grandson offered the site to Trinity Church for a new Episcopal house of worship. St. Mark's was begun in 1795 and largely finished in 1799, making it the second oldest church in Manhattan, after St. Paul's Chapel. The steeple was added by Ithiel Town in 1828 and the cast-iron portico in 1854.

St. Mark's became a free-wheeling outpost in the 20th century, drawing performers and worshipers like W. H. Auden, Ted Berrigan, Isadora Duncan, Allen Ginsberg, Martha Graham, Robert Lowell, Sam Shepard and Edna St. Vincent Millay. Its rector, the Rev. Michael J. C. Allen, was known as the "hippie priest." And it was home to Theater Genesis, one of the first Off-Off-Broadway coffeehouse theaters. In 1974, the long-running Danspace Project was inaugurated here.

Fire ravaged the church in July 1978. Under the Rev. David A. Garcia, the building was restored over the following five years, to designs by the Edelman Partnership. The rectory, at 232 East 11th Street,

was rebuilt in 1999 to provide offices for a number of preservation groups, as well as an apartment for the rector.

On Sunday, Lectio Divina (Bible study), is offered at 9:30 a.m., followed by a general worship service at 10:15, with child care and Sunday school available. The vespers at 6:30 p.m. on Wednesday include a celebration of the Eucharist and silent meditation.

Church of the Immaculate Conception
406 East 14th Street, near First Avenue
Designated landmark

A little colony of French Gothic buildings constructed from 1894
to 1896 as Grace Church's mission chapel, and acquired in the
1940s by a Roman Catholic parish. Barney & Chapman were the
architects. Note the inscription on the fountain in the 14th Street
façade: "Ho, everyone that thirsteth" (Isaiah 55).

St. John's in the Village
224 Waverly Place, at West 11th Street
Within a historic district

This Episcopal church was built from 1972 to 1974 to replace
an earlier sanctuary on the same site that had burned down.
The architect Edgar Tafel evoked both the Greek Revival style
and the massing of the original, in a modern vernacular.

Church of St. Joseph
365 Avenue of the Americas, at Washington Place
Within a historic district

A robust Greek Revival temple designed by John Doran
and built from 1833 to 1834 for a parish that still worships
here. It is the oldest Roman Catholic church built as such
in New York City.

Washington Square
United Methodist Church
133 West Fourth Street, near Washington Square West
Within a historic district

Housed in an 1860 Gothic Revival sanctuary by Charles Hadden
is the "Peace Church," a congregation so progressive that it
offered sanctuary to soldiers refusing military service in the
Persian Gulf War.

Chelsea, Madison Square and Vicinity

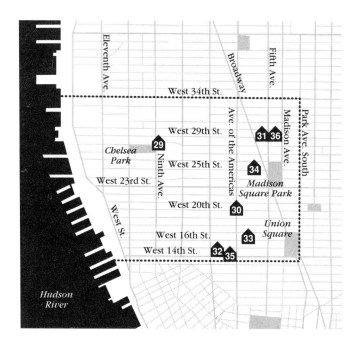

29 Church of the Holy Apostles
30 Limelight
31 Marble Collegiate Church
32 Church of Our Lady
of Guadalupe
33 Church of St. Francis Xavier

34 St. Sava Serbian
Orthodox Cathedral
35 Salvation Army Centennial
Memorial Chapel
36 Church of the
Transfiguration

Church of the Holy Apostles

296 Ninth Avenue,
at West 28th Street
(212) 807-6799
www.holyapostlesnyc.org

Designated landmark

Holy Apostles is a Chelsea icon, its soaring steeple undiminished by the towers around it. But the high profile of this Episcopal church has as much to do with its embrace of those who are unwelcome elsewhere, a tradition that may be traced to the days before the Civil War, when the church was reputed to have been a stop on the Underground Railroad.

The soup kitchen, begun in 1982, serves anyone who comes to the door. That can mean about 1,000 meals a day (for a total of 4 million meals as of mid-2000). Holy Apostles was also the first home, from 1973 to 1975, of Congregation Beth Simchat Torah, the gay and lesbian synagogue.

This was probably not quite the future imagined in 1836 by the founders of a Sunday school from which Holy Apostles emerged. The church, by Minard Lafever, was built from 1846 to 1848. Though a contemporary of Trinity Church, it is not Gothic but northern Italian in spirit. William Jay Bolton, who worked with Lafever on the first major stained-glass commission in the United States, at the Church of the Holy Trinity in Brooklyn, created windows that are striking in their bold, geometric pattern.

Just as a new roof was being finished in April 1990, fire broke out, badly damaging the church and destroying six sections of the Bolton windows. But under the Rev. William A. Greenlaw, the church began a heroic second restoration, directed by Ed Kamper, and reopened in 1994. The nave was transformed into a flexible space that is now used for the soup kitchen.

The Rev. Ellen Barrett, the first woman priest in the Episcopal diocese of New York, was ordained here in 1977. A former deacon at Holy Apostles, the Rt. Rev. Catherine S. Roskam, was consecrated in 1996 as the first woman bishop in the diocese.

Sunday services at 11 a.m. include the full choir. The Eucharist is offered Tuesday at 6:15 p.m., with a healing service on the first Tuesday of every month. Congregation Beth Simchat Torah, (212) 929-9498 or www.cbst.org, is temporarily using the church again for its 8 p.m. Friday services and community Sabbath dinners at 6 p.m.

Limelight

47 West 20th Street,
at the Avenue of the Americas
(212) 807-7780
Designated landmark

More famous—or infamous—for what it became than what it was, one of New York's longest-running nightclubs is housed in the charming former Episcopal Church of the Holy Communion, designed by Richard Upjohn and finished in 1846, the same year as his Trinity Church on Wall Street.

Anna C. Rogers built the church in memory of her husband, whose dying wish was for a house of God to be established "where rich and poor might meet together." Her brother, the Rev. William A. Muhlenberg, was the first pastor. A sisterhood at the church ran St. Luke's Hospital when it was at Fifth Avenue and 54th Street. The Easter Parade is said to have evolved from the custom of bringing flowers to patients there. In 1883 the church was the host of the first convocation of black Episcopal clergymen.

Holy Communion merged with the Calvary and St. George's parishes in 1976. The deconsecrated building was thereafter used by Odyssey Institute as a drug rehabilitation center. Odyssey sold the building to an impresario named Peter Gatien, who opened Limelight in 1983 with a party at which Andy Warhol was the host. One guest was reportedly carried in on a cross. "This is public depravity I have never thought possible, even in New York," lamented Bishop Paul Moore Jr. of the Episcopal Diocese. Linked by law-enforcement authorities to widespread drug trafficking, Limelight was closed by the police in 1996. But Gatien reopened it in 1998, much to the neighbors' consternation.

Marble Collegiate Church

1 West 29th Street,
at Fifth Avenue
(212) 686-2770
www.marblechurch.org

Designated landmark

Looking like a Romanesque pile of sugar cubes, Marble was designed by Samuel A. Warner and built from 1851 to 1854 as the Fifth Avenue Church. Its glistening stones imprinted themselves on the civic consciousness, however, and the building material officially gave its name to the congregation in 1906.

Marble is one of four bodies under a single consistory—composed of elders, deacons and ministers—that governs the Collegiate Reformed Protestant Dutch Church of the City of New York. Organized in 1628, it describes itself as the oldest Protestant denomination in America with a continuous ministry. (The other members of the consistory are the Fort Washington, Middle and West End churches.) Ministers in this denomination once shared the several pulpits collegially. In 1871, however, they stopped preaching in rotation and each was given his own congregation.

In the 20th century, few pulpits and preachers were as intertwined as Marble and the Rev. Norman Vincent Peale, one of America's most influential religious figures. Called to Marble in 1932, Peale was among the first clergymen to bring psychological counseling to his flock, working with Dr. Smiley Blanton, a psychiatrist trained by Sigmund Freud. Peale was also a pioneer in the use of radio and television in his ministry. But most famously, he was the author of *The Power of Positive Thinking*. (In later years, Peale identified Donald J. Trump, whose family is closely associated with Marble, as "one of America's top positive thinkers.")

After Peale retired in 1984, the Rev. Arthur Caliandro succeeded to the pulpit. In the late 1990s the church undertook a major exterior restoration, designed by the Hall Partnership, and it installed its first new stained-glass window in nearly a century, by Lamb

Studios. (Earlier ones, by Frederick Wilson for Louis Comfort Tiffany, were installed in 1900 and 1901.) Reflecting Marble's image as an inclusive community, the window panel depicting the Pentecost shows three children: Asian, black and white.

Sunday is a very busy day at Marble. Before the 11:15 a.m. service, nursery and child care is available. Then there is the "10 o'clock hour" for adults, as well as church school, choirs for all ages and brunch. But the church is active every day, with lunches for the elderly, art fellowship meetings and spirituality workshops.

Church of Our Lady of Guadalupe

229 West 14th Street, near Seventh Avenue (212) 243-5317

Once known as Little Spain, West 14th Street is home to the oldest Spanish-speaking congregation in New York, Nuestra Señora de Guadalupe, honoring the patron of Mexico, whose appearances in 1531 to Juan Diego, an Indian who had embraced Christianity, led to the conversion of millions.

The parish was founded in 1902 by, and is still in care of, an order known as the Augustinians of the Assumption. The façade was added in 1921 to an existing row house and brings a touch of Spanish Baroque to 14th Street, with its rounded pediment and iron porch. The architect, Gustave Steinback, was responsible for the much grander Church of the Blessed Sacrament on West 71st Street. Inside, the sanctuary's hand-painted walls vividly recall the churches of Latin America.

Over time, as the composition of New York's Hispanic community changed, Our Lady of Guadalupe has served Spaniards, Spanish-Americans, Puerto Ricans and Mexican immigrants.

On Saturday evening, Sunday and holy days, Masses are in Spanish. There are also Masses in English, Monday through Saturday.

Church of St. Francis Xavier

30 West 16th Street,
near the Avenue of the Americas
(212) 627-2100
www.rc.net/newyork/stfrancisxavier/

Exuberantly complex, a bit offbeat and impossible to ignore—that is true of both the architecture and the Jesuit-run Roman Catholic parish itself. The church and adjoining Xavier High School were founded in 1847. The present sanctuary, by Patrick C. Keely, was built from 1878 to 1882. Its great Baroque domed crossing is one of the more dramatic spaces in any New York church.

At the forefront of social change, the church housed the Xavier Institute of Industrial Relations, which offered courses for union members in labor relations, law and welfare programs until 1988. Priests and graduates of the institute helped longshoremen and tunnel workers fight union corruption and establish honest elections. It was led by the Rev. Philip A. Carey, known as the "Sandhog Priest." Another member of the institute, the Rev. John M. Corridan, was the model for the rough-and-tumble Father Barry, played by Karl Malden in the 1954 movie *On the Waterfront*.

In 1979 the church began offering a special weekly Mass for members of Dignity, a group of gay and lesbian Roman Catholics, but was ordered in 1987 by the Archdiocese of New York to discontinue the services.

Sunday Masses begin Saturday at 5 p.m. and continue Sunday at 9, 10:15 (in Spanish), 11:30 and 5. There are three weekday Masses and one on Saturday, and a healing liturgy once a month.

St. Sava
Serbian
Orthodox
Cathedral

15 West 25th Street,
near Broadway
(212) 242-9240
members.aol.com/saintsava

Designated landmark

When wealthy uptown communicants of Trinity Church needed a more convenient place to worship, they simply built one. Trinity Chapel, constructed from 1851 to 1856, was designed by Richard Upjohn, the architect of the mother church, though in a more delicate, proto-Victorian kind of Gothic, complemented by Jacob Wrey Mould's Trinity Chapel School, which was built next door in 1860.

Edith Jones, a celebrated chronicler of upper-class society, was married in the lofty sanctuary in 1885, taking the name of her husband, Edward Wharton. But the old-time gentry had long since departed by 1942, when the building was sold to the fledgling Serbian Eastern Orthodox Church of St. Sava, dedicated to the first archbishop and patron saint of the Serbs. The church was consecrated in 1944 under the Rev. Dushan Shoukletovich. King Peter II, the last king of Yugoslavia, attended services here.

Gradually, the building has been remade from a Protestant chapel to an Orthodox cathedral. In 1962 an oak iconostasis carved at a monastery in South Serbia was added. Byzantine-style windows were commissioned to replace those destroyed when a bomb went off nearby at the Communist Party headquarters on 26th Street in 1973. The gilded bust outside is of Bishop Nikolai Velimirovich, who helped organize the Serbian Orthodox Church in America and was in later years the "luminary-in-residence" at the cathedral, unable to return to his homeland under Marshal Tito.

Long a center of Serbian life in New York, the cathedral held prayer services in the 1990s "for the victims of the brutal NATO aggression against the Serbian people."

Services are conducted every Sunday from 10:30 a.m. until 12:30 p.m. There are prayer services every night at 6:30.

Salvation Army Centennial Memorial Temple

120 West 14th Street,
near the Avenue of the Americas
(212) 337-7200
www.salvationarmy-newyork.org

Yes, these are the uniformed folks with the bells and red buckets at Christmastime, but the Salvation Army is more than a worldwide social-service agency. It is also a Christian denomination, founded by William Booth in 1865 as the East London Christian Mission. Its unusual name derives from a declaration in its 1878 annual report that "the Christian Mission is a Salvation Army."

George Scott Railton brought the Army's missionary work to New York in 1880. In 1929 work began on the Salvation Army's national headquarters, a complex designed by Ralph Walker, of Voorhees, Gmelin & Walker, who was a master of the Ziggurat Moderne style.

Within the complex is a 1,600-seat auditorium called the Centennial Memorial Temple, as 1929 was the 100th anniversary of Booth's birth. The project was supervised by Booth's daughter, Evangeline, who was the Army's commander in the United States. She managed every detail, including the installation of larger seats every fourth or fifth aisle for overweight soldiers. The hall is also notable for clusters of lighting recessed behind willowlike screens. The exterior presents a grand entry arch framed by walls whose low-relief folds look almost like parting curtains.

Although its national headquarters moved out in 1981, the Salvation Army still conducts meetings in this hall at 7:30 p.m. every other Friday, and the public is invited. The temple is available for special events and is also used for services by evangelical groups, such as the Word of Life.

Church of the Transfiguration

1 East 29th Street,
near Fifth Avenue
(212) 684-6770
www.littlechurch.org

Designated landmark

In 1870, refusing a funeral for George Holland—one of those "morally questionable" actors—the Rev. William T. Sabine of the Episcopal Church of the Atonement at Madison Avenue and East 28th Street told one of Holland's friends, Joseph Jefferson: "I believe there is a little church around the corner where they do that sort of thing." "If that be so, sir," Jefferson replied, "God bless the little church around the corner."

Around the corner, at Transfiguration, the Rev. George H. Houghton welcomed the actors. They have been coming ever since to the Little Church Around the Corner. In the 1920s the rector, the Very Rev. J. H. Randolph Ray, helped found the Episcopal Actors' Guild, whose members included Tallulah Bankhead, Rex Harrison and Charlton Heston. In the 1970s, the church housed the Joseph Jefferson Theatre Company, with such up-and-coming actors as Armand Assante, Tom Hulce and Rhea Perlman.

The church building itself is no less a star. Built in 1850, it expanded over the years in a random sort of way that earned it the nickname "Holy Cucumber Vine." This beloved, picturesque complex has a pretty garden and the distinctive feature of a lich gate, a roofed pavilion at the entrance to a churchyard, where a corpse is to be set down before being taken inside. This lich gate, designed by Frederick Clark Withers in 1896, serves more as a quiet waystation for the living.

Transfiguration is noted for long rectorships: only five in a century and a half. And as for the very upright Church of the Atonement, that parish dissolved in 1880 and its building is long gone.

The church is open on Sunday and holidays. Weekday services are conducted in the adjoining chapel, which is open all day.

Chapel of the Good Shepherd
at the General Theological Seminary
175 Ninth Avenue, at West 21st Street
Within a historic district

Crowning the lovely Close—a picturesque 19th-century quadrangle that is worth a visit in any event—is this Gothic chapel and bell tower, built from 1886 to 1888 and designed by Charles Coolidge Haight, whose father was the first rector of St. Peter's Church (next entry).

St. Peter's Church
344 West 20th Street, near Ninth Avenue
Within a historic district

It was supposed to be Greek Revival, like the chapel at No. 346, designed by Clement Clarke Moore, but this 1838 Episcopal church wound up as an early work of Gothic Revival, with a severe tower that looks more ancient than it is. James W. Smith was the architect.

Gramercy Park, Stuyvesant Square and Kips Bay

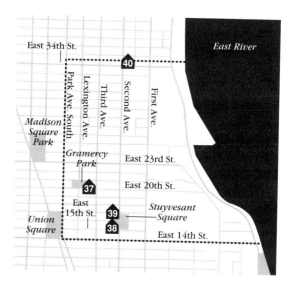

37 Brotherhood Synagogue
38 Fifteenth Street Friends
   Meeting House

39 St. George's Church
40 St. Vartan Armenian
   Cathedral

Brotherhood Synagogue

28 Gramercy Park South,
near Third Avenue
(212) 674-5750
brotherhoodsynagogue.org

Designated landmark

"The theme of our Synagogue is love, its message is brotherhood, its tool is the Bible, its aim is peace, its program is fellowship," said Rabbi Irving J. Block on the night in 1954 that he founded Beth Achim (House of Brothers), a Conservative congregation better known as the Brotherhood Synagogue. And peaceful indeed is the prospect of this Italianate meeting house, glimpsed from under the verdant canopy around Gramercy Park.

But serenity doesn't tell the whole story, since this sanctuary was born of two distinct rifts. The first was in 1828, when a schism occurred among the otherwise-peaceable Quakers, who divided into orthodox and liberal branches. New York's orthodox Friends built this structure, designed by King & Kellum, from 1859 to 1860. They were here almost a century before rejoining the liberal group at the Fifteenth Street Meeting House.

The second rift occurred in 1973, when the Brotherhood Synagogue parted from the Village Presbyterian Church, with which it had been sharing a sanctuary on West 13th Street (now the Portico Place apartment house). The congregation purchased the old Gramercy Park meeting house and remodeled it. James Stewart Polshek designed the renovation and, later, the adjacent Garden of Remembrance, an austere little oasis that opened in 1982 as a memorial not only to family members and friends but also to those who perished in the Holocaust.

Brotherhood's services, 6:30 p.m. on Friday and 9:30 a.m. on Saturday, encourage "congregational involvement and the equal participation of men and women." Among the special services for children is a Toddler Shabbat. The temple is always open to anyone for prayer. An education program includes courses in Judaism and Hebrew.

Fifteenth Street Friends Meeting House

15 Rutherford Place,
at East 15th Street
(212) 777-8866
metroquakers.org

Designated landmark

So plain that it now looks beautiful, the Quakers' Fifteenth Street meetinghouse was built on Stuyvesant Square in 1861 for the liberal followers of Elias Hicks, who separated from the orthodox Friends in the schism of 1828. (The latter group built what is now the Brotherhood Synagogue.) Charles T. Bunting is credited as the architect of the meetinghouse and adjacent seminary, at 226 East 16th Street. Made of red brick, with the simple pediment and gabled roof of the Greek Revival, the design reflects a form of worship that brooks no ostentation or distraction, is free of symbols, and begins in silence, without formal liturgy. The Friends Meeting House in Flushing, Queens, which dates to 1694, is the oldest existing house of worship in New York City.

Meetings are held on Sunday at 9:30 and 11 a.m. and on Wednesday at 6:30 p.m. A small Mennonite group also worships here.

St. George's Church

209 East 16th Street,
at Rutherford Place
(212) 475-0830
e-mail: parishsec@aol.com

Designated landmark

L ooming grandly over Stuyvesant Square, this Episcopal church brings a sturdy timelessness to a neighborhood that has undergone much transformation. Built from 1846 to 1848, St. George's was one of the first Romanesque Revival churches in New York. At the time, the more ornate Gothic style was in wide favor. It may have been that the Rev. Stephen H. Tyng, who belonged to the evangelical branch of Episcopalianism known as Low Church, sought to distinguish his sanctuary architecturally from the fancy High Church parishes.

St. George's was founded in 1749, while New York was still a colony, as a chapel of Trinity Church. When it stood on Beekman Street, it was the site of the first commencement for King's College, now Columbia University.

In 1811 St. George's became a freestanding parish. Its church on Stuyvesant Square was designed by Leopold Eidlitz and Otto Blesch in a southern German style. For a time, the interior was the largest in the city. A fire in 1865 badly weakened its twin steeples, which were taken down in 1889.

J. P. Morgan became a warden in 1885 and remained one until his death in 1913. His funeral drew a crowd estimated at 30,000.

St. George's merged in 1976 with two nearby parishes: Holy Communion (whose building is now the Limelight nightclub) and Calvary Church, 273 Park Avenue South, at East 21st Street, which was designed by James Renwick Jr. and completed in 1848. Under the Rev. Thomas F. Pike, St. George's was one of the first churches in New York to house the homeless, beginning in 1982.

The only service now conducted in the sanctuary is at 11 a.m. on Sunday, with a choir. The 8:30 and 10 a.m. services are conducted in the chapel. St. George's is closed at other times, and most activities take place at Calvary Church.

St. Vartan Armenian Cathedral

630 Second Avenue,
at East 34th Street
(212) 686-0710
www.fordham.edu/halsall/medny/stvartan1.html

A gold-leaf conical dome atop a great drum, rising 140 feet over Second Avenue, makes St. Vartan unlike any other house of worship in Manhattan, though it is strikingly similar to the great churches of Armenia, including the 1,500-year-old Cathedral of Holy Etchmiadzin.

Armenia, which once extended from the Mediterranean to the Caspian to the Black Sea, was the first country to adopt Christianity as a state religion, in 301. A century and a half later, St. Vartan Mamigonian was slain in battle defending the faith. He is the namesake of this cathedral and can be seen in relief over the entrance, with a helmet at his feet.

The campaign to erect this remarkable structure was led by Archbishop Sion Manoogian, primate of the eastern diocese, and his successor, Archbishop Torkom Manoogian, who later became the Armenian Patriarch of Jerusalem. Designed by Steinmann & Cain, the cathedral was built from 1966 to 1968, borrowing not only from Etchmiadzin but also from the ninth-century church of Aghtamar. It was consecrated by Vasken I, Supreme Patriarch and Catholicos of All Armenians.

Inside, visible through wheel-shaped chandeliers, the dome is adorned at its center with an Armenian letter representing the expression "He is." One of the eight ornamental medallions around the

dome contains a symbol familiar from the $1 bill: an eye in a triangle, emblem of an all-seeing God, the trinity within one.

The cathedral is open Monday through Friday, 10 a.m. to 6 p.m. On Sunday, common prayers are recited at 9:30 a.m. and the divine liturgy is at 10:30. If the main door to the cathedral is locked during visiting hours, admittance can be gained through the office.

Community Church of New York

40 East 35th Street
Designated landmark

This red-brick box is an early International style sanctuary,
designed for the nondenominational church by Magoon & Salo
and built from 1940 to 1948. (World War II occasioned the long
interruption in construction.) It is also the home of the Metropolitan
Synagogue of New York.

Church of the Incarnation

209 Madison Avenue, at East 35th Street
Designated landmark

Spare and sober on the outside but with stained glass and sculptural
treasures inside, this Gothic Revival church was designed by
Emlen T. Littel and completed in 1865 for the Episcopalian parish
that still uses it.

Church of Our Lady
of the Scapular/St. Stephen

149 East 28th Street, near Third Avenue

Erupting like a fountain, with a great round pediment from which
the rest of the façade cascades, this Roman Catholic church was
designed by James Renwick Jr. and completed in 1855. It contains
murals by Constantine Brumidi, whose work ornaments the dome
of the United States Capitol.

Midtown, Times Square and Clinton

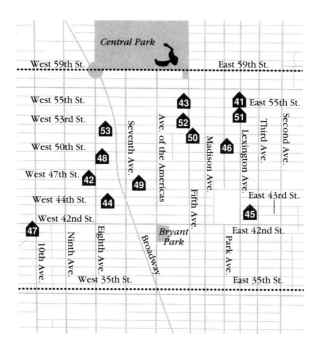

41 Central Synagogue
42 Congregation Ezrath Israel
43 Fifth Avenue Presbyterian Church
44 John's Pizzeria
45 Church of St. Agnes
46 St. Bartholomew's Church
47 Church of SS. Cyril and Methodius/St. Raphael's Church

48 St. Malachy's Church
49 Church of St. Mary the Virgin
50 St. Patrick's Cathedral
51 St. Peter's Church
52 St. Thomas Church
53 Times Square Church

Central Synagogue

652 Lexington Avenue,
at East 55th Street
(212) 838-5122

Designated landmark

Using Moorish architecture to proclaim itself vibrantly and exuberantly different from Gentile churches, this venerable Reform synagogue is notable for its twin octagonal minarets, topped by copper globes, and its bichromatic horseshoe arches, flanking a rose window with a ten-pointed star tracery. Inside, it was—if possible—even more exotic, with intricate, scintillating Moorish-style stenciling on every surface that isn't otherwise carved in black walnut, covered in encaustic tile or shaped into cusped arches.

Designed by Henry Fernbach and constructed from 1870 to 1872, Central is the oldest synagogue in New York still in use by the congregation that built it. Ahawath Chesed (Love of Mercy) was founded on Ludlow Street in 1846 by German-speaking Bohemian immigrants. It merged in 1898 with Congregation Shaar Hashomayim (Gates of Heaven), a German group founded in 1839 on Attorney Street.

In August 1998, as a renovation of Central Synagogue neared completion, a fire blazed through the roof and gutted the sanctuary, though it spared the Ark. "We will take our Torah scrolls, which we have, and we will wander for a period of time, and then in a great triumphant moment, we will return to that building," promised the senior rabbi, Peter J. Rubinstein. On High Holy Days that year, the congregation worshiped in the Seventh Regiment Armory on Park Avenue after Gov. George E. Pataki suspended a ban on religious

observances in public spaces. The congregation has since undertaken a $38 million restoration and renovation, by Hardy Holzman Pfeiffer Associates, that is to be completed in 2001.

During reconstruction of this landmark, services are being held across the street at the community house. Sabbath is celebrated at 5:45 p.m. on Friday and 10 a.m. on Saturday; weekday services are at 8 a.m., Monday through Thursday, and 7:45 a.m. on Friday. The Judaica Museum, housed in the same building, is open from 9 a.m. to 4:30 p.m., Monday through Friday. Admission is free.

Congregation Ezrath Israel

339 West 47th Street,
near Eighth Avenue
(212) 245-6975

So modest that it could almost be mistaken for a small annex to the school next door, this synagogue is actually a more typical house of worship than the high-style landmarks that dominate a visitor's agenda. Its significance, indeed, is not at all architectural. Rather, it is the home of a Conservative congregation, Ezrath Israel (Help of Israel), also known as the Actors' Temple. It began ministering to actors in the 1920s, under Rabbi Bernard Birstein. Although it was on the outskirts of the theater district, Ezrath Israel had not even allowed actors to say kaddish here. Changing that policy, Birstein told Sophie Tucker: "I want actors to come to us, to feel welcome for a change. I want it to be their shul." Jack Benny, Milton Berle, Red Buttons, Eddie Cantor, Oscar Levant and Henny Youngman were among the many who responded to that invitation over the years. So were the brothers Jerome and Harry Moses Horwitz, Curly and Moe of the Three Stooges. They came here to say kaddish.

Services are on Friday at 6:30 p.m. and Saturday at 9 a.m., as well as mornings and evenings daily.

Fifth Avenue Presbyterian Church

7 West 55th Street,
at Fifth Avenue
(212) 247-0490
www.fapc.org

Agreat Victorian gingerbread castle with a tower more than 20 stories high, this church remains every bit the cynosure it was on completion in 1876. Like Trinity Church downtown, it holds its own against its skyscraping neighbors. It is the largest Presbyterian sanctuary in Manhattan, with the largest congregation, numbering more than 3,000.

The congregation was founded on Cedar Street in 1808. Its members included Archibald Gracie, whose country home on the East River is now the mayoral residence. The congregation moved to Duane and Church Streets in 1836, then to Fifth Avenue and 19th Street in 1852. Its current sanctuary was designed by Carl Pfeiffer and was begun in 1873. Although it is Gothic on the outside, its interior—at the insistence of the Rev. John Hall—was laid out as a radiant amphitheater in which pews flow from the pulpit. It has been said that there is not a right angle to be found in the room, which can seat 1,800. The woodwork was by Kimbel & Cabus and the stained glass by John C. Spence. A 10-story Church House, designed by James Gamble Rogers, was added in 1925.

Sunday services are at 9 and 11 a.m., complete with the formidable organ that was renovated in 1999, the Fifth Avenue Choir and, occasionally, the Children's Choir. The Center for Christian Studies is an educational program that runs from September to May, with courses in the Bible, theology, church history and the arts.

John's Pizzeria

260 West 44th Street,
near Eighth Avenue
(212) 391-7560

W hat is now the main dining room of a popular theater-district restaurant began as the sanctuary of the Gospel Tabernacle, a religious revival house that once packed them in as tightly as any hit show on Broadway. Until his death in 1919, it was the pulpit of the Rev. Albert B. Simpson, founder of the Christian Alliance. This charismatic preacher could raise $50,000 for the missions during a single meeting, despite the fact that his was  probably Manhattan's least visible church, located in the center of the block, surrounded by other buildings, with no discernible façade except two inconspicuous Gothic doorways. (They can still be seen on Eighth Avenue, between 43rd and 44th Streets.)

Inside was the large sanctuary with a balcony, under a joyous, honey-colored octagonal stained-glass skylight. In the 1980s the space became the Chapel of the Crucifixion as part of Covenant House, a Roman Catholic organization founded by the Rev. Bruce Ritter to help runaway teenagers. In 1997 the chapel was transformed by the architect Andrew Tesoro and the muralist Douglas Cooper into John's Pizzeria. The sanctuary is now the main dining room. So, while waiting for a pizza with your favorite topping, be sure to look up and admire the one above you.

Church of St. Agnes

141 Archbishop Fulton J. Sheen Place
(East 43rd Street),
near Third Avenue
(212) 682-5722

One of Manhattan's newest houses of worship is one of its most traditional in design, befitting its conservative pastoral and political role. Completed in 1998 and designed by Acheson, Thornton, Doyle, it is a pared-down limestone version of the 16th-century Il Gesù in Rome.

St. Agnes, one of a handful of Roman Catholic churches in which the Latin Mass known as the Tridentine Rite is celebrated, was founded in 1873 to serve Irish laborers working on the Grand Central Depot nearby. Its first church, a Victorian Gothic building with twin towers, was designed by Lawrence J. O'Connor and completed in 1877. Eamon de Valera, who would later serve as prime minister and president of Ireland, was baptized here in 1882. Archbishop Fulton J. Sheen, known for his radio and television broadcasts, preached here for 50 years. It was from this church that Cardinal John J. O'Connor led an anti-abortion march in 1992.

A haven for both commuters and the homeless, St. Agnes was destroyed in a December 1992 fire that claimed the sanctuary, the roof, the choir window and the newly restored Aeolian-Skinner organ. Two looters trying to take gold candelabra were stopped by Rudolph W. Giuliani, not yet the mayor, who happened by even before firefighters were on the scene.

The pastor, Msgr. Eugene V. Clark, vowed to rebuild. And he kept his promise.

The Tridentine Mass is celebrated at 12:30 p.m. on Sunday. There are six other Masses on Sundays, five on Saturdays and seven on weekdays. A small bookstore is to the right of the sanctuary.

St. Bartholomew's Church

109 East 50th Street,
at Park Avenue
(212) 378-0200
www.stbarts.org

Designated landmark

Years have passed since the battle for St. Bart's ended. Wounds are healing. The church is recovering. Attendance is rising and deficits are falling. But the fight over one of the most valuable parcels of real estate in New York is likely to resonate for many more years as a defining moment in the history of the Episcopal parish. That is no small thing, since St. Bartholomew's goes back to 1835, when it was organized on Lafayette Street.

In 1876 it moved to a striking Lombardic structure by James Renwick Jr. at Madison Avenue and 44th Street. An elaborate triple portal, designed by Stanford White and inspired by the Benedictine abbey of St. Gilles-du-Gard in Provence, was added to the church in 1902. In 1905 St. Bart's brought Leopold Stokowski to the United States to serve as its organist. But the Rev. David H. Greer also saw to it that the church ministered to the poor, at its parish house on East 42nd Street.

When the congregation moved uptown, White's portal came along and served as the starting point for the design of the new church, built from 1917 to 1919. But Bertram Grosvenor Goodhue did much more than provide a setting for the portal. He applied the same brilliant synthesis of ancient and modern forms, this time in a Byzantine-Romanesque style that he had so successfully used in Gothic churches like St. Thomas. Other great artists involved in St. Bart's were Daniel Chester French, Philip Martiny and Hildreth Meiere. The golden-hued sanctuary occupies the north half of the full-block lot, its marble mosaic dome nearly 150 feet high. On the south side are a garden and a community house that continues the work of the 42nd Street parish house.

In the 1980s, under the Rev. Thomas D. Bowers, a divided congregation sought to replace the community house with a 47-story office tower. "Our mission is to somehow use the resources we have to the maximum extent possible to touch human lives," Bowers said.

But the Landmarks Preservation Commission said that the tower would compete with, minimize, trivialize and confuse the meaning of the landmark. A legal battle began that lasted until 1991, when the Supreme Court refused to hear St. Bart's constitutional challenge to the landmark designation.

St. Bart's is nothing if not a full-service church, beginning with worship services seven days a week, 365 days a year. Four Eucharistic services are held on Sunday, when free parking and child care are available. There are musical programs for all tastes, courses in adult and religious education, a bookstore, food programs, social clubs, a counseling center, prayer circles, a sailing club, a community theater and a docent program that conducts tours of the building after the 11 a.m. service every Sunday.

Church of SS. Cyril and Methodius / St. Raphael's Church

508 Cardinal Stepinac Place
(West 41st Street),
near Tenth Avenue
(212) 563-3395
e-mail: crkvanyc@aol.com

Watching over the Lincoln Tunnel like a twin-peaked Gothic fortress crested with copper crosses, this grand Roman Catholic church was built in 1914 to designs by George A. Streeton. As St. Raphael's, a parish founded in 1886, it served the Irish of Hell's Kitchen. Young Daniel Patrick Moynihan worshiped and cast his first vote here. In 1974 it also began to function as a home for a Croatian Roman Catholic parish, and the names of Cyril and Methodius, the apostles of the Slavs, were added. (Cardinal Alojzije Stepinac, for whom this stretch of 41st Street was renamed, was archbishop of Zagreb in World War II.) Under the Rev. Slavko Soldo, the church was a hub of Croatian relief efforts in the 1990s, during the fighting in the former Yugoslavian state. The Croatian Center is directly adjacent, on 40th Street. The original SS. Cyril and Methodius Church of 1913 still stands at 552 West 50th Street.

Masses are celebrated in Croatian at 9 and 11 a.m. on Sundays and in English at 10 a.m. Weekday Masses are in English at 7:30 and Croatian at 8 a.m.

St. Malachy's Church

239 West 49th Street,
near Eighth Avenue
(212) 489-1340

Its chimes once played "There's No Business Like Show Business" and the Rev. George Washington Moore Jr., who helped save it in the 1970s, was awarded a special Tony. This Roman Catholic parish, known as the Actors' Chapel, has been identified with Broadway ever since the 1920s, when it was the setting for the funeral of Rudolph Valentino and for the wedding of Douglas Fairbanks Jr. to Joan Crawford (or "Le Sueur, Lucile," as her name is given in the church register). Worshipers over the years here have  included Fred Allen, Don Ameche, George M. Cohan, Perry Como, Irene Dunne, Sir Alec Guinness, Bob Hope, Florence Henderson, Pat O'Brien, Carol O'Connor, Rosalind Russell, Danny Thomas and Spencer Tracy.

St. Malachy's occupies a neo-Gothic sanctuary designed by Joseph H. McGuire that was built in 1903 and restored in 1993. Every September, this church, Congregation Ezrath Israel (the Actors' Temple), St. Luke's Lutheran and St. Clement's Episcopal all take part in an interdenominational service called the "Broadway Blessing," to pray for the new theater season.

St. Malachy's is open from 7:30 a.m. to 5 p.m. weekdays. There is music at the 5 p.m. Mass on Saturday. A choir sings at the 11 a.m. service on Sunday, and the liturgy is in Portuguese at 1 p.m. The church founded and sponsors Encore Community Services (212) 581-2910, a nonsectarian agency helping the elderly.

Church of
St. Mary the Virgin

139 West 46th Street,
near Seventh Avenue
(212) 869-5830
www.stmvirgin.com

Designated landmark

D on't let that Gothic masonry fool
you. St. Mary was a structural
pioneer in the 1890s: one of the first
churches—if not *the* first—built with a
skeletal steel framework.

Steel was useful because the building
had to carry a heavy symbolic load. If
you did not know this was an Episcopal
church, you'd think it was Roman
Catholic. St. Mary is a leader in Anglo-
Catholicism, the ritual-rich evocation of
pre-Reformation liturgy and architecture.
The use of heavy incense here inspired
the irreverent nickname "Smoky Mary's."

The parish was founded in 1867. The 46th Street sanctuary,
Lady Chapel, clergy house, mission house and rectory were built
from 1894 to 1895 to designs by Napoleon LeBrun & Sons, architects
of St. Cecilia's Roman Catholic Church on East 106th Street. The
sculptures are by John Massey Rhind. The installation of the
Aeolian-Skinner organ, one of the first designed by G. Donald
Harrison, was begun in 1932 but not completed until in 1995.

From 1996 to 1997, under the Rev. Canon Edgar F. Wells, the
church underwent a restoration designed by J. Lawrence Jones &
Associates of Brooklyn. The 80-foot-high ceiling was painted deep
blue with golden stars. To step under that sky is to leave Manhattan's
tumult far behind.

**The church is open Monday through Friday, 7 a.m. to 9 a.m. and 11
a.m. to 7 p.m.; Saturday, 11 a.m. to 5:30 p.m.; and Sunday, 8 a.m. to 6
p.m. Masses are said every day, with four on Sunday. A small gift shop
off the foyer is open on weekends. Excellent acoustics make listening to
the organ and the many choral programs a pleasure.**

St. Patrick's Cathedral

625 Fifth Avenue,
at East 50th Street
(212) 753-2261
www.ny-archdiocese.org/pastoral/
cathedral_about.html
Designated landmark

If this guidebook had only one entry, it would surely be St. Patrick's Cathedral. Because of its place in the heart of mid-Manhattan, because of its size and its beauty, and because of the power and influence its bishops have long enjoyed, St. Patrick's is the very image of the Roman Catholic church in America. It comes as close as any single religious institution to being synonymous with New York. "It happens to transcend all faiths," said Edward I. Koch, who was mayor during the cathedral's centenary in 1979.

For Archbishop John J. Hughes, who conceived it, the cathedral was to stand for the "increasing numbers, intelligence and wealth" of the Catholic community and to serve as a "public architectural monument of the present and prospective greatness of this metropolis of the American Continent." Both goals were realized. St. Patrick's fills a city block: 332 feet long and 174 feet wide. It seats 2,500 people but can accommodate many, many more.

Begun on a lot that was supposed to be a cemetery, so far out of town that it was called "Hughes's Folly," St. Patrick's has seen a metropolis grow around it. It was the first church in the United States to be visited by a reigning pope, Paul VI, in 1965, followed 14 years later by Pope John Paul II.

Long before the popes arrived, St. Patrick's had strong ties to the Old World, not only as an emblem of Ireland, to whose patron it is dedicated, but as a 19th-century version of great European cathedrals, most notably those of Reims and Cologne. James Renwick Jr., the architect of Grace Church, designed the cathedral, as well as the parish house and archbishop's residence that flank its eastern end. He was assisted by William Rodrigue, Hughes's brother-in-law.

The cornerstone was laid in 1858, but the cathedral was not formally consecrated and opened until 1879, construction having been interrupted by the Civil War. By 1888, the 330-foot towers were finished. Nineteen bells, manufactured by Paccard of Annecy, France, were installed in 1897.

Between 1901 and 1906, the Lady Chapel, by Charles T. Matthews, was added to the east end. Parts of the wall removed from

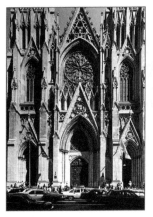

the cathedral were incorporated into the Church of Our Lady of
Lourdes, at 467 West 142nd Street.

The three great windows are the 26-foot-diameter rose, with
stained glass by Charles Connick of Boston; the "Life of St. Patrick,"
or titular window, in the south transept, by Henry Ely of Nantes,
France, and the "Life of the Blessed Virgin," north transept, by
Nicholas Lorin of Chartres.

The bronze doors, designed by Charles D. Maginnis, with statues
by John Angel, were added in 1949. The cathedral has been renovated and artistically enriched several times. The copper statue of Our
Lady, by Anthony Minervini, was added in 1978 to the roof of the
Lady Chapel.

In striking contrast to the Gothic ambience are the modern
shrines of St. Elizabeth Ann Seton, by Frederick Shrady (1975), and
St. John Neumann, by Herbert Gunther (1977), which includes a rep-
resentation of St. Patrick's Old Cathedral downtown.

And what are those scarlet disks hanging from the ceiling, looking like wide-brimmed hats with tassles? That's exactly what they are:
"galeros," emblems of the cardinals who lie buried beneath them
in the crypt: John McCloskey, the first American cardinal, who
celebrated the cathedral's dedication Mass; John M. Farley, who
finished the Lady Chapel; Patrick J. Hayes; and Francis J. Spellman,
who consecrated a new main altar in 1942. The galero emblem is
no longer used, so there are none for Terence J. Cooke, who died
in 1983, or John J. O'Connor.

O'Connor, who became a cardinal in 1985, publicly deplored the
idea of the archbishopric as "Powerhouse," but he was in fact a most

influential political leader. The spires of St. Patrick's occasionally seemed more like lightning rods during his tenure, but O'Connor used the cathedral so effectively as bully pulpit that the identities of man and institution merged. When he missed his first St. Patrick's Day Mass, two months before his death in May 2000, a retired police officer noted sadly: "He was the spark plug that made it move." O'Connor was succeeded by Bishop Edward M. Egan of Bridgeport, Conn.

The cathedral is open from 7 a.m. to 8:45 p.m. There are eight Masses on Sunday (the high Mass is at 10:15), eight each day of the week, and five on Saturday, including the 5:30 vigil. Various devotional services are held at 6 p.m. every day. There is a small gift shop in the cathedral and a large store across 51st Street, at No. 15.

St. Peter's Church

619 Lexington Avenue,
at East 54th Street
(212) 935-2200
www.saintpeters.org

It seems somehow fitting that a commercial real estate transaction paved the way for what may be New York's best postwar church. St. Peter's is not flawless, but it is an ambitious and largely successful attempt to create a serene, voluminous, contemplative spiritual space in a modern vernacular, with little resort to conventional or traditional liturgical design or iconography.

This Lutheran congregation was founded in 1861 and worshiped on Lexington Avenue and 46th Street. It was uprooted for the Grand Central Terminal complex and received a settlement that helped it build a Victorian Gothic church at Lexington and 54th Street in 1903. By the late 1960s, the church was pondering a sale of its property. Brokers got wind of that and figured that the lot might be the start of an assemblage for a new headquarters of the First National City Bank. In 1970 the bank agreed to pay St. Peter's $9 million for its building and to construct the shell of a new church on its old site, with most of the block taken up by the 59-story Citicorp Center, now called Citigroup Center.

The new St. Peter's, finished in 1977 under the pastorate of the Rev. Ralph E. Peterson, was designed by Hugh Stubbins & Associates, architects of Citicorp Center. Stubbins described the polygonal shape, clad in gray granite and cleft by a glass channel, as "two hands held up in prayer with light coming between them." The church calls it a "majestic rock, a stable monument that affirms God's presence," likening the sanctuary, below sidewalk level, to the inside of a granite tent. The interior was designed by Vignelli Associates, with an organ by the Johannes Klais Orgelbau of Bonn. Louise Nevelson created a suite of sculptural elements, all in white, that adorn the walls of the intimate Erol Beker Chapel of the Good Shepherd.

Not far from the jazz clubs on 52nd Street (before they disappeared), St. Peter's was celebrated for three decades as the home of the Jazz Pastor, the Rev. John Garcia Gensel, who inspired "The Shepherd Who Watches Over the Night Flock" by Duke Ellington. Knowing that musicians were not likely to make a Sunday morning gig, Gensel held jazz vespers at 5 p.m. Asked whether such services might attract a bad element, he replied: "That's the kind we want in church. The good ones can stay home. A church is a congregation of sinners, not an assembly of saints."

St Peter's has four services on Sunday: Masses in English at 8:45 and 11 a.m., in Spanish at 1:30 and jazz vespers at 5 p.m. This combination of uniquely American music with the Christian liturgy is one of a number of musical programs the church offers. It also has a choir that performs classical concerts.

St. Thomas Church

1 West 53rd Street,
at Fifth Avenue
(212) 757-7013
www.saintthomaschurch.org

Designated landmark

Though it long ago lost most of the Gilded Age mansions that gave its name a fabled ring, Fifth Avenue still boasts some the grandest houses of worship in America. St. Thomas Episcopal is one of them.

The congregation, founded in 1823, was no less conspicuous at Broadway and Houston Street. Its first church, completed in 1826 to designs by Joseph R. Brady and the Rev. John McVickar, was an early forerunner of Gothic Revival, with octagonal towers that rose over the surrounding countryside. The parish moved uptown to its current location in 1870. Its brownstone church by Richard Upjohn was destroyed by fire in 1905.

The replacement church, built from 1911 to 1916, was the last that Ralph Adams Cram and Bertram Grosvenor Goodhue designed in partnership. It combines the best of their strengths: Cram's spiritual embrace of pure Gothicism—as he insisted, the church is built entirely of masonry, without supporting steel—and Goodhue's forceful and daring manipulation of the form to suit a modern environment. A second glance is needed to realize that this seemingly formal Gothic façade is in fact daringly asymmetrical, with a single corner tower. The church underwent a restoration, designed by Beyer Blinder Belle, beginning in 1996.

As striking as the exterior is Goodhue's great reredos behind the altar, 80 feet high, with 60 figures carved by Lee Lawrie, including George Washington and William E. Gladstone. By Cram's estimation, St. Thomas was probably "the most expensive church per square foot" built in the United States and the quality is evident throughout. Surely, it's no accident that St. Thomas is the church of the high-society Seton family in the movie *Holiday* (1938), nor did a stonecarver's addition of a dollar sign over the bride's door on Fifth Avenue pass unnoticed. But the parish is also involved in inner-city ministry. All Saints' Church at 230 East 60th Street, once a dead-end part of town, was a mission church of St. Thomas until 1963. It is now independent.

Music is at the heart of parish life. The St. Thomas Choir School, a boarding school for boys in the fourth through eighth grades, was founded in 1919 at the instance of T. Tertius Noble, organist and choirmaster. Its new building at 202 West 58th Street was completed in 1987.

The church is open from 7 a.m. to 5:30 p.m. every day. One can take a tour with the aid of a pamphlet available in the vestibule, or with a guide after the 11 a.m. service on Sunday. The choir can be heard September through April at the five principal worship services each week, or at Tuesday evening concerts. For information on concerts, call (212) 664-9360 or e-mail concerts@saintthomaschurch.org.

Times Square Church

237 West 51st Street,
near Broadway
(212) 541-6300
www.tscpulpitseries.org/tsc.html

Designated landmark

Times Square was near its nadir in 1986 when the Rev. David Wilkerson, an evangelist and the author of *The Cross and the Switchblade*, founded this nondenominational, fundamentalist, Pentecostal Christian church. It began in Town Hall, moved to the Nederlander Theater and now occupies the former Mark Hellinger Theater.

Wilkerson followed a long tradition of using theaters as religious sanctuaries. In Harlem, for example, the legendary Lafayette Theater became the Williams Institutional Christian Methodist Episcopal Church, the Regent Theater became the First Corinthian Baptist Church and Loew's 116th Street Theater became the Canaan Baptist Church.

The Mark Hellinger Theater opened in 1930 as the Warner Hollywood, one of the last great movie palaces, designed by Thomas

W. Lamb and the Rambusch Studios. Though the exterior is stark Deco-Secessionist, inside is an unbridled Baroque fantasy. In its days as a Broadway venue, it housed the long-running *My Fair Lady* and—perhaps an augury of sorts—*Jesus Christ Superstar.*

The Times Square Church now draws 6,000 to 8,000 people each Sunday, many of whom overflow into an annex on Broadway and follow the service on closed-circuit TV. As the area draws more and more tourists, the church finds itself playing host to groups who came only long enough to hear the lively choir. It is trying to find ways to get them to stay longer.

Services at the Times Square Church are held at 10 a.m., 3 p.m. and 6 p.m. on Sunday and at 7 p.m. on Tuesday and Friday. There is a prayer service on Thursday at 7 p.m.

Some other notable houses of worship in the area:

Actors Studio
432 West 44th Street, near 10th Avenue
Designated landmark

Perhaps New York's last Greek Revival church, this appealingly simple brick building was constructed in 1859. It was known as the West 44th Street Presbyterian Church before Lee Strasberg's Actors Studio took over in 1955.

Church For All Nations
417 West 57th Street, near Ninth Avenue

Recalling somewhat the work of Frank Furness, a most inventive Victorian Gothic architect, this sanctuary was built in 1885 to designs by Francis Hatch Kimball for the Catholic Apostolic Church. It was acquired in 1995 by the Lutheran congregation that now uses it.

Holy Cross Church
333 West 42nd Street, near Ninth Avenue

A great dome, nearly 150 feet high, distinguishes this 1870 sanctuary by Henry Engelbert. This was the pulpit of the Rev. Francis P. Duffy, chaplain to the "Fighting Irish" regiment in World War I and namesake of Duffy Square at Broadway and 46th Street. A statue of Duffy by Charles Keck stands vigilantly there, before a great granite Celtic cross.

Lincoln Square
and Vicinity

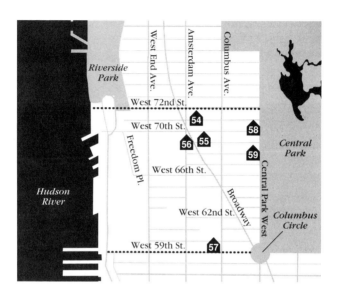

54 Church of the Blessed Sacrament

55 Christ and St. Stephen's Church

56 Lincoln Square Synagogue

57 Church of St. Paul the Apostle

58 Congregation Shearith Israel

59 Stephen Wise Free Synagogue

Church of the Blessed Sacrament

152 West 71st Street, near Broadway (212) 877-3111

The soaring Gothic nave, the ranks of statuary and the vast rose window are monumental enough to terminate a grand axis in Paris. But Blessed Sacrament sits in mid-block, waiting to surprise—even overwhelm—passersby.

Founded in a stable in 1887 the parish built a brick church on this site, with a little schoolhouse on Broadway. William Tecumseh Sherman, who marched the Union forces to the sea during the Civil War, lived down the block. The pastor of Blessed Sacrament officiated at his funeral service in 1891.

In 1917 the architect Gustave Steinback designed the present church on an extraordinary scale. You will be struck by the great rose window, designed by Clement Heaton, and by the enormous tympanum over the main portal, with a relief based on Raphael's *The Triumph of the Eucharist*. By all means go inside to marvel further at the vast clerestory windows, ribbed vaults and clustered columns, which look like something more out of St. Patrick's than a parish church.

Blessed Sacrament sold its Broadway parcel in 1922 to the developers of the Hotel Alamac, now an apartment building, the construction of which considerably diminished the visibility of the church.

Masses begin on Saturday at 5:30 p.m., followed on Sunday at 8, 9:15, 11 a.m. (in Spanish), 12:30 (with choir) and 5:30 p.m. There is a Family Mass on Sunday at 10:15 a.m., followed by religious instruction. Weekday Masses are said at 7:30 a.m., 12:10 and 5:30 p.m.. The church is open until the completion of the 5:30 Mass.

Christ & St. Stephen's Church

120 West 69th Street,
near Broadway
(212) 787-2755
www.csschurch.org

Stand on West 69th Street, close your eyes and think of the Little Church Around the Corner, a picturesquely haphazard design of nooks and crannies, set well off from the street behind a screen of trees and shrubbery. Open your eyes again and here it is: the suburban chapel of the Church of the Transfiguration.

It was built in 1876 under the rectorship of the Rev. George H. Houghton, the one who welcomed actors to the East 29th Street sanctuary. William H. Day was the architect of the uptown chapel. The windows, most of them by the London firm Heaton, Butler & Bayne, are among its treasures.

The sanctuary was remodeled by J. D. Fouquet and acquired in 1897 by St. Stephen's Episcopal parish. Its arrival in the neighborhood did not please Christ Episcopal Church, which had settled a few years earlier in a Romanesque building by Charles Coolidge Haight at Broadway and 71st Street. Christ Church sued St. Stephen's for infringing on parish boundaries. In the 1970s, however, the two parishes—by then badly depleted, in part from the loss of hundreds of parishioners displaced by the construction of Lincoln Center—joined together under the Rev. Joseph Zorawick.

The old Christ Church was truncated in 1925 for a commercial development at 2061 Broadway, the eight-story Lester Building. The remaining mid-block portion of the sanctuary was used by the Bible Deliverance Evangelical Church before it was finally razed in the 1980s. A ghost image of the nave, in cross section, can be seen on the rear wall of the Lester Building from the plaza in front of the Lincoln Park apartments.

Holy Eucharist is celebrated on Sunday at 8:30 and 11 a.m.; Wednesday at 12:15 p.m. Morning prayers are on Tuesday, Wednesday and Friday, 8:30 a.m.; evening prayers on Monday, Wednesday and Thursday, 5:15 p.m. The best light on the windows, the church points out, is right after the 11 a.m. Sunday service. The Adonai Arts Foundation sponsors concerts here, from children's piano recitals to operas.

Lincoln Square Synagogue

200 Amsterdam Avenue,
at West 69th Street
(212) 874-6100
www.lss.org

When you sit in this sanctuary-in-the-round, you may feel everyone is looking at you. But that is part of the design: to emphasize unity. The curving structure, clad in travertine and inscribed with a verse from Isaiah 44 ("Return to me for I have redeemed you"), was designed by Hausman & Rosenberg and built in 1970.

This leading Orthodox congregation was founded in 1964 by Rabbi Shlomo Riskin, who attracted a crowd missed by so many houses of worship: young, professional and intellectual. Today some 1,000 families and individuals belong. In 1998, under Rabbi Adam Mintz, Lincoln Square took the pioneering step for an Orthodox synagogue of appointing a woman, Julie Stern Joseph, to share the rabbi's responsibilities as a "congregational intern."

Lincoln Square is within the Upper West Side eruv, which stretches from West 61st to West 107th Streets and from Central Park West to the West Side Highway (now the Joe DiMaggio Highway). This area represents a symbolic extension of a private home, in which observant Jews are allowed to carry objects or to push their children in strollers, activities that would otherwise be proscribed on the

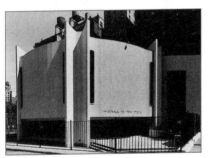

Sabbath. The eruv is defined both by the walls of existing buildings and, where necessary, by translucent fishing line at treetop level. It was erected by Lincoln Square and Congregation Ohab Zedek, 118 West 95th Street.

This very active synagogue conducts a number of Sabbath services beginning on Friday evenings. On Saturday, minyans begin at 7:45 a.m. and continue at 9 a.m. in the main sanctuary, at 9:15 for newcomers, and 9:45 for young people. Morning and evening services are offered every day. There is an extensive religious-education program aimed at the entire family.

Church of
St. Paul
the Apostle

405 West 59th Street,
at Columbus Avenue
(212) 265-3495
www.stpaultheapostle.org

This treasure house of ecclesiastical art was once the second-largest church in the nation, after St. Patrick's Cathedral. It is still awfully imposing, with its massive rough-hewn towers, built from stones that once formed the Croton Aqueduct. The Paulist Fathers, the Roman Catholic order whose church this is, even called it Fort Deshon, after its designer, the Rev. George Deshon, who taught engineering at West Point before becoming a priest.

Within the 284-foot basilican interior are Stanford White's gleaming, golden hemispherical canopy, rising on eight columns of colored porphyry stone over a smaller gilded dome above the altar; Bertram Grosvenor Goodhue's robustly modern floor mosaics, installed in 1920, one of which depicts the Acropolis as St. Paul would have beheld it from the Hill of Mars; and a suspended sanctuary lamp by Philip Martiny, which appears to be held up in the interlocked hands of four angels. The stars painted in the ceiling depict the celestial alignment on January 25, 1885, when the church was dedicated. The bas relief outside, designed by Lumen Martin Winter in 1958, shows the conversion of St. Paul. Winter also designed the monumental Angel of the Resurrection, under which the Rev. Isaac Thomas Hecker is buried. Hecker, a New Yorker who was acquainted with Transcendentalism, converted to Catholicism at the age of 24, became a Redemptorist missionary and then founded the Paulist order in 1858.

The church is open every day from early morning until 6 p.m. From September to April, it is open Sunday until the end of the 9 p.m. Mass. There is a bookstore and gift shop.

Congregation Shearith Israel

8 West 70th Street,
at Central Park West
(212) 873-0300
www.shearith-israel.org

Designated landmark

Like towering architectural counterpoints to the oaks across the
street, four great Corinthian columns dominate the façade of this
elaborate Orthodox synagogue. And the neo-Classicism is more than
skin deep. Even the Ark, carved in tawny Sienna marble and framed
by butter-yellow Tiffany windows, has the broad pediment and
Corinthian columns of Greco-Roman architecture.

Congregation Shearith Israel (Remnant of Israel) doesn't go back
quite that far. But it is the oldest Jewish congregation in North
America. Shearith Israel traces itself to a group of 23 Jews, mostly
Spanish and Portuguese, who came here from Recife, Brazil, in 1654.

The oldest remaining physical trace of Shearith Israel is the tomb-
stone of Benjamin Bueno de Mesquita, who died in 1683 and is
buried in the congregation's tiny Chatham Square cemetery downtown, on St. James Place, sharing the block with St. James Church.
The second cemetery, established in 1805, still exists as a tiny patch
on West 11th Street, just east of the Avenue of the Americas. The third
cemetery, of 1829, can be found on West 21st Street, just west of the
Avenue of the Americas.

Shearith Israel's earliest synagogues stood on Mill Street, now
known as South William Street. Its sons fought in the American
Revolution and one of its Torah scrolls was desecrated by the British
during the occupation. Until 1825, Shearith Israel was the only synagogue in New York.

The congregation moved to Crosby Street in 1834 and to West
19th Street in 1860. Though these synagogues are long gone, the former residence of the reader, or hazzan, still stands at 7 West 19th Street.

Shearith Israel's present sanctuary, on Central Park West, was built
from 1896 to 1897 and designed by Brunner & Tryon. Contemporary
discoveries of synagogue ruins in Galilee from the Greco-Roman period
had stoked a neo-Classical boomlet in synagogue architecture, lending
what the architect Arnold W. Brunner called the "sanction of antiquity."

Antiquity is further celebrated in the Little Synagogue of the
1897 building, which was designed in Colonial style to emulate the
earlier homes of Shearith Israel and includes furnishings from the
1730 synagogue.

Though the entrance to the building appears to be on Central Park West, the Ark is actually behind that monumental arcade. It was placed at the eastern wall so that congregants facing it in prayer would also face Jerusalem. The entrance is instead on the western end, reached from 70th Street.

In 1998, under Rabbi Marc D. Angel, Shearith Israel undertook a restoration of its windows by the Clerkin Higgins Stained Glass studio. "When you come into the synagogue, you realize you're in the presence of God," Angel said. "You feel the span of the centuries." You can even hear the span of the centuries, since the creaking floor boards under the reader's platform are said to have come from the Mill Street synagogue.

In addition to Sabbath observances, conducted with a professional choir participating, prayer services are held every morning and evening. All prayers are read in Sephardic Hebrew. There is a learner's service every Saturday at 9:30 a.m. The congregation sponsors religious, educational and cultural programs. Its archives go back to colonial times.

Stephen Wise Free Synagogue

30 West 68th Street,
near Central Park West
(212) 877-4050
www.swfs.org

Within a historic district

Though houses of worship are sometimes informally known by the name of their rector, rabbi or pastor, it rarely happens that a congregation formally and permanently identifies itself with an individual. But Rabbi Stephen Samuel Wise was in every sense synonymous with the Free Synagogue, a Reform congregation that he founded in 1907.

Wise also founded the Jewish Institute of Religion, the Zionist Organization of America and, with Louis Brandeis and Felix Frankfurter, the American Jewish Congress. He was rabbi of

Congregation B'nai Jeshurun from 1893 to 1900, but turned down an invitation in 1905 to the pulpit of Emanu-El when he was told that he would be subject to control by the board of trustees. "How can a man be vital and independent and helpful, if he be tethered and muzzled?" Wise asked. "A free pulpit will sometimes stumble into error; a pulpit that is not free can never powerfully plead for truth and righteousness."

Wise then began conducting services just three blocks from Emanu-El, in the Hudson Theater at 139 West 44th Street (now preserved and incorporated into the Millennium Broadway Hotel). The Free Synagogue was founded in 1907 to be free and democratic in its organization—"pewless and dueless," in the words of its first president, Henry Morgenthau Sr.

The Free Synagogue built a neo-Gothic sanctuary at 40 West 68th Street from 1922 to 1923, designed by Eisendrath & Horowitz. Its 600-seat auditorium could not contain the crowds that came to hear Wise, however, so services were conducted in Carnegie Hall. A new synagogue designed by Bloch & Hesse, with more than twice the capacity, was begun next door at No. 30 in 1940. The building at

No. 40 was subsequently used by the Jewish Institute of Religion and is now the York Preparatory School, though it still bears a plaque that says, "Free Synagogue House."

Rabbi Balfour Brickner was perhaps the best known of Wise's successors, as an outspoken voice in the 1980s for abortion rights, civil rights and the environment, and against U.S. involvement in Central America and corporate investment in South Africa.

Reflecting the liberal, socially progressive tenor set by the founder, the synagogue remains active in community programs, feeding 75 homeless men and women every Sabbath morning, running a 10-bed homeless shelter and feeding, clothing and counseling AIDS patients.

The Sabbath is observed in the sanctuary every Friday night at 8, except on the first Friday of the month, when there is a family service with the junior choir at 7:30 p.m., and on the last, when there is a "3D" service—davening, dinner and discussion—at 6. Saturday begins with Torah study at 9:45 a.m. and a service at 11. Child care is available at all services and a 10 a.m. Tot Shabbat is held monthly. Each year, the synagogue co-sponsors the Judith Raskin Memorial Concert, featuring the winners of the Metropolitan Opera's national auditions.

Church of Jesus Christ of Latter-day Saints
125 Columbus Avenue, at West 65th Street

This huge travertine-clad box was built in 1975 as part of
Two Lincoln Square, designed by Schuman, Lichtenstein & Claman.
Its chief attraction to the public is the Family History Center
(212) 873-1690, where anyone can trace family geneaology
at no charge. The center is open from 10 a.m. to 8 p.m.,
Tuesday through Friday, and to 5 p.m. on Saturdays.

Upper West Side and Morningside Heights

60 Congregation B'nai Jeshurun
61 First Baptist Church
62 First Church of Christ,
Scientist
63 Fourth Universalist Society
64 Holy Trinity Church
65 Riverside Church

66 Congregation Rodeph
Sholom
67 Rutgers Presbyterian Church
68 Cathedral Church of
St. John the Divine
69 Church of St. Paul and
St. Andrew
70 West End Collegiate Church

Congregation
B'nai Jeshurun

257 West 88th Street,
near Broadway
(212) 787-7600
www.bj.org

Within a historic district

Not so much a jewel box as a jewel mine, glowing, gilded and festooned with interwoven geometric ornament, the interior of this synagogue—part Coptic, part Moorish, part Persian—is far richer than its exterior would lead you to believe. And the history of the Conservative congregation is richer still.

It is second in age only to Shearith Israel, from which B'nai Jeshurun (Sons of Israel) split in 1825. In the early 19th century, immigrants from Germany, Poland, Holland and England first worshiped at Shearith Israel—the only synagogue in town—despite the differences between the Ashkenazic ritual to which they were accustomed and the Sephardic order of service used at the Spanish and Portuguese congregation. When they were rebuffed in their attempt to conduct separate services, however, they broke with the older group and secured their own sanctuary on Elm Street.

B'nai Jeshurun moved over time to Greene Street; to West 34th Street, where Macy's now stands; then to 746 Madison Avenue, near 65th Street, a Spanish-Moorish temple designed by Schwarzmann & Bachmann and Rafael Guastavino, completed in 1885. It was home to the congregation when Stephen S. Wise was rabbi. Radically altered, the Madison Avenue building still stands. You can see the arched windows of its side walls in the middle of the block.

The present synagogue was built from 1917 to 1918 and designed by Walter S. Schneider and Henry B. Herts Jr. in what they called a truly "Semitic character," to prove that synagogues need not be "servile copies of Mohammedan mosques" or "ape the prevalent styles of Christian churches or Pagan temples."

As one of the city's most influential synagogues, B'nai Jeshurun drew speakers like Eleanor Roosevelt and Martin Luther King Jr. But when Marshall T. Meyer arrived as the rabbi in 1985, having been the outspoken leader of the largest synagogue in Buenos Aires, he had to count himself and his wife to create a minyan. Meyer set out to infuse the moribund congregation with a moral and social purpose. He reached out to young singles, to homeless people, to Christians and Muslims. Meyer died in 1993 but his dynamic leadership of

"BJ," as the congregation is fondly called by its members, was continued by Rabbis J. Rolando Matalon and Marcel R. Bronstein, both from Argentina.

Services were moved to the nearby Church of St. Paul and St. Andrew after the ceiling collapsed in 1991. The congregation was able to return five years later but continues to use the church as its 3,000 members and hundreds more visitors can scarcely be accommodated in a sanctuary built for 1,100.

Sabbath services in the synagogue are held at 6 p.m. on Friday and 9:30 a.m. on Saturday. There is a second Friday service at 6:45 p.m. in the Church of St. Paul and St. Andrew, 263 West 86th Street. There is a daily morning minyan at 7:30, Monday through Friday, and at 9:30 on Sunday. Members are encouraged to participate in programs helping the sick, the elderly, the homeless and the environment.

First Baptist Church

265 West 79th Street,
at Broadway
(212) 724-5600

With the Apthorp apartments to the south and Zabar's to the north, a house of worship has to do something to stand out. First Baptist does, embracing this vital intersection as if with outstretched arms, its broad entryway set diagonally on the corner.

Organized in 1745 on Gold Street, First Baptist moved over time to Broome Street and then to East 39th Street. From 1890 to 1893, under the Rev. Isaac M. Haldeman, it built the present church, designed by George Keister. The sanctuary is most unusual in that the long axis runs at a 45-degree angle to the surrounding streets. (All Angels' Episcopal Church, built at exactly the same time only a block away, set its sanctuary diagonally to get the maximum length possible on the site.) First Baptist is graced with a barrel-vaulted skylight that runs the length of the ceiling. Unfortunately, it was covered over long ago.

The most arresting feature of the façade is the asymmetrical towers. These are no accident. The south tower, which stands in its entirety, symbolizes Christ. Its shorter and deliberately unfinished companion to the north represents the Christian community as it awaits Christ's return.

The 11 a.m. Sunday service is preceded by a Sunday school for adults and children. There are prayer meetings and Bible study on Wednesday at 6:20 p.m. and Saturday at 10:30 a.m. The sanctuary stays open every Monday, Tuesday and Thursday night for meditation and consolation.

First Church of Christ, Scientist

11 West 96th Street,
at Central Park West
(212) 749-3088
www.csnyc.com/manhattan.html

Designated landmark

Augusta Emma Stetson could have stopped with this landmark and been remembered as one of New York's great church builders. But she had even bigger dreams.

She was dispatched from Boston in 1886 by Mary Baker Eddy, the founder of Christian Science, to sow the seeds of the faith in New York. She organized the First Church of Christ, Scientist, the following year. By 1903 Stetson was able to open—debt free—this imposing structure by Carrère & Hastings, architects of the New York Public Library on Fifth Avenue, with a central window by John La Farge. It is at once a steeple-topped New England meetinghouse, a neoclassical temple and a Mannerist work in the style of the British architect Nicholas Hawksmoor. More than just an enormous sanctuary—the auditorium can seat 2,400—the building also includes a Christian Science reading room.

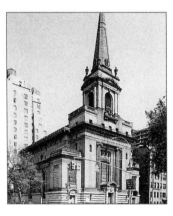

That would have been accomplishment enough for many church leaders, but Stetson boldly conceived a Christian Science Church in New York to rival the Mother Church in Boston. When Eddy got wind of this, she made her displeasure known. In 1909 Stetson was forced to resign her membership in the First Church.

The landmark building has faced hard times of its own in recent years, as the congregation has dwindled to a fraction of its original size and vandals broke the stained-glass windows and marred the Concord granite walls with graffiti.

Sunday services and Sunday school are at 11 a.m.; Wednesday evening testimony meetings at 7:30. The reading room is open Monday through Saturday and on Wednesday evening until 7:15.

Fourth Universalist Society

160 Central Park West,
at West 76th Street
(212) 595-1658
www.fourthuniversalist.org

Within a historic district

Its architectural profile is pure 15th century—an icicle-delicate tower straight out of Magdalen College, Oxford—but its spiritual profile is very 20th century. The Unitarian Universalist Association, formed in 1961 by the consolidation of the Universalists and the Unitarians, describes itself as a noncreedal, liberal religion born of Jewish and Christian traditions.

The forerunner of this congregation was the Universalist Church of the Divine Paternity, founded in 1838. Traveling uptown over the decades, it moved into a sanctuary on Broadway that had been vacated the Unitarian Church of the Divine Unity, which is now called All Souls and is the "UU" congregation across town.

This lovely Perpendicular Gothic sanctuary was completed in 1898 to designs by William A. Potter, with an altar by Louis Comfort Tiffany, relief sculpture by Augustus St. Gaudens and stained glass by Clayton & Bell of London.

Courted by developers in the 1980s for its enormously attractive site, the society instead formed a neighborhood alliance called SOUL—Save Our Universalist Landmark—in which the community pledged to help raise the money needed for repairs and maintenance while the church agreed not to exercise its development rights.

Principal services are on Sunday at 11 a.m. The society has an ambitious music program under Kenneth Hamrick and offers professional classical and jazz performances. Other programs include "Dream Catchers," an exploration of conscious dreaming techniques, and "Moon Circle," an earth-centered ritual and sharing group.

Holy Trinity Church

213 West 82nd Street,
near Amsterdam Avenue
(212) 787-0634
www.fordham.edu/halsall/medny/taylor1.html

A vast dome of herringboned Guastavino tiles suggests the vaults of the Oyster Bar at Grand Central Terminal. But it also evokes the interior of Hagia Sophia in Istanbul, as intended by the Rev. Michael J. Considine, during whose pastorate this Roman Catholic church was built from 1910 to 1912. (The parish itself dates to 1898.) The architect was Joseph H. McGuire, who was also responsible for St. Malachy's in the theater district. Inscribed on the Byzantine façade is the minor doxology: Glory to the Father, the Son and Holy Spirit. Copper cupolas atop the façade were removed in 1995. But at the same time, the inside of the 66-foot-diameter dome was re-illuminated to grand effect.

Sunday Masses are at 11 a.m. (in Spanish), 12:30 p.m. (with choir) and 5:30 p.m. (with choir). Weekday Masses are at 9 a.m. and 5:30 p.m.

Riverside Church

490 Riverside Drive,
at West 122nd Street
(212) 870-6700
www.theriversidechurchny.org

Designated landmark

No church in New York commands a more spectacular site than this one, visible for miles from a bluff overlooking the Hudson River. The architecture makes the most of its privileged spot, with a 392-foot skyscraping tower that houses 22 floors of church rooms and the 74-bell Laura Spelman Rockefeller Memorial Carillon. The view from its observation deck is not to be missed.

In religious and social programs, Riverside is every bit as prominent as its architecture. Even Fidel Castro has spoken here, at the end of the United Nations millennial summit in 2000. Riverside calls itself an "interdenominational, interracial and international" congregation of 2,400 members and affiliates, allied with both the United Church of Christ and the American Baptist Churches. Its senior minister since 1989 has been the Rev. James Alexander Forbes Jr., who succeeded to the pulpit of the Rev. Harry Emerson Fosdick and the Rev. William Sloane Coffin Jr.

The neo-Gothic church was built from 1927 to 1930 as a result of the conflicts between the liberal and fundamental wings of Protestantism. Fosdick resigned as associate pastor of the First Presbyterian Church in 1925 after two failed attempts led by William Jennings Bryan to oust him. John D. Rockefeller Jr., dissatisfied with what he perceived as a lack of ecumenism at St. John the Divine, put up $8 million to finance an interdenominational church for the charismatic Fosdick.

The congregation at the nucleus of this new institution was the Park Avenue Baptist Church, descended from the Norfolk Street Baptist Church (now the Beth Hamedrash Hagodol synagogue). The Park Avenue church, at East 64th Street, was designed by Henry C. Pelton and Allen & Collens of Boston. (It is now the Central Presbyterian Church.)

Allen & Collens were the architects of Riverside, which originally consisted only of the sanctuary and tower, modeled loosely on Chartres Cathedral. The addition, designed by Collens, Willis & Beckonert and now known as the Martin Luther King Jr. Wing, was not completed until 1955, on the site of what had been a privately owned miniature golf course.

In 2000, the Landmarks Preservation Commission designated the sanctuary and tower a landmark, though some in the congregation believed that the new wing also warranted landmark status. This was a far cry from 1931, when an essay in *The American Architect* magazine ridiculed the choice of 13th-century motifs for a pulpit occupied by a modern churchman like Fosdick, huffing, "We would not require Gershwin to perform and compose on a harpsichord."

The Sunday service is at 10:45 a.m. On Tuesday there is a meditation service called "Walking the Labyrinth" at 6 p.m. and on Wednesday informal worship at 7 p.m. The carillon is open Tuesday through Sunday and can be heard on Sunday afternoons. The observation deck is open to the public. Information and tickets to these and many other events, including one of the most active music programs in the city, can be obtained at the visitors center and gift shop.

Congregation Rodeph Sholom

7 West 83rd Street,
near Central Park West
(212) 362-8800
www.uahc.org/congs/ny/ny038/

Within a historic district

"Walk humbly with thy God," command the words from the Book of Micah, inscribed across the façade of this Reform synagogue. But a little bit of pride is surely in order, since Rodeph Sholom (Pursuers of Peace) is one of the oldest congregations in New York.

German immigrants founded the congregation in 1842. In early years, it was loosely federated with two other German groups, Anshe Chesed (a predecessor of Emanu-El) and Shaar Hashomayim (which became the Central Synagogue). The three congregations shared one of New York's first ordained rabbis, Max Lilienthal.

Rodeph Sholom built a Romanesque synagogue at 8 Clinton Street, near Houston Street, in 1853, with two stair towers to the women's galleries. Not only does this building survive, it is still used as a synagogue by Congregation Chasam Sopher (Seal of the Scribe), an Orthodox group.

After a spell on Lexington Avenue and on East 63rd Street, Rodeph Sholom built the present synagogue from 1929 to 1930, dedicating it at the festival of Purim. The architect, Charles B. Meyers, also designed Congregation Ohab Zedek, at 118 West 95th Street. Unlike many synagogues of the 1920s that had a single monumental portal in their façades, Rodeph Sholom has three tremendous arched windows, making it a powerful presence on a quiet side street off Central Park.

Gunter Hirschberg, an aspiring opera singer who came here as the cantor, was named senior rabbi in 1972. He founded the first Reform Jewish day school in the 1970s. In 1991, to celebrate Rodeph Sholom's sesquicentenary, Rabbi Robert N. Levine and 75 congregation members retraced on foot the six-mile uptown odyssey from Clinton Street to West 83rd Street. "We wanted to feel a sense of our roots," Levine explained. They run very deep.

Sabbath services are held at 6 p.m. on Friday and 10:15 a.m. on Saturday. There is a lay-led minyan on Wednesday at 6:30 p.m.

Rutgers Presbyterian Church

236 West 73rd Street,
near Broadway
(212) 877-8227
www.rutgerschurch.com

Does Rutgers ring a bell? It should, for this church and the State University of New Jersey are both namesakes of Col. Henry Rutgers, who fought in the Revolutionary War and farmed on the Lower East Side. He gave a parcel of his estate to an adjunct congregation of the First Presbyterian Church that was founded in 1798. The Rutgers congregation, as it came to be known, built two sanctuaries, at Rutgers and Henry Streets, before moving uptown. (The second church is used to this day by St. Teresa's Roman Catholic parish.)

In 1890 the Rutgers congregation erected a handsome Romanesque church by R. H. Robertson at the corner of Broadway and West 73rd Street. But after three decades, it leased this valuable corner site to a bank, and moved to the middle of the block, into a far more modest sanctuary, that was built from 1921 to 1926 and designed by Henry Otis Chapman. To those who believed the church had mixed up its priorities, the Rev. Daniel Russell explained: "It is no more than a question of putting real estate values, which are lying idle, to work for the kingdom of God." The investment continues to pay dividends, as the church today is a hub of social-service activity in the neighborhood.

The church is open from 10 a.m. to 4:45 p.m., Monday through Friday. Sunday worship is at 11 a.m. Child care is available. Rutgers offers meals for the elderly and a weekend shelter for homeless men.

Cathedral Church of St. John the Divine

1047 Amsterdam Avenue,
at West 112th Street
(212) 316-7540
www.stjohndivine.org

Divine is not an adjective here; it is a noun, meaning St. John the Theologian. And "divine" would not do justice to the saga of the world's largest Gothic cathedral. Like a Hollywood spectacular, it is stupendous and gorgeous to behold. But it has a melodramatic sub-plot that twists and turns without ever reaching a conclusion.

In the 1880s, while the towers of the new Roman Catholic cathedral were rising on Fifth Avenue, the Episcopal bishop of New York, Henry Codman Potter, decided to build something even greater. The 13-acre campus of the Leake and Watts Orphan Asylum, on a bluff overlooking the Harlem plain, suggested itself as the site of a modern acropolis, formed by the cathedral, Columbia University and St. Luke's Hospital. (The asylum itself, an 1843 Greek Revival building designed by Ithiel Town, still stands and today houses the cathedral's Textile Conservation Laboratory.)

George L. Heins and Grant La Farge, who would go on to design the stations of the original subway system, won an architectural competition in 1891 with their plan for a Romanesque building with a huge spire over the crossing.

Construction began December 27, St. John's Day, in 1892. The project quickly ran into foundation problems, but J.P. Morgan, a cathedral trustee, gave $500,000 "to get us out of the hole." The design was on even shakier ground. From the outset, the trustees had wanted a more Gothic look, and in 1907, after the death of Heins, they turned to the ultimate Gothicist, Ralph Adams Cram.

The implementation of Cram's design began in 1916. The building was extended to 601 feet ("two football fields end to end," it was said, "with room left for the football"). Then came the west front, followed by the baptistry and part of the north transept. Finally, on Sunday, November 30, 1941, the opening of the entire 16,822,000-cubic-foot interior was celebrated. Construction abruptly ceased, however, after the following Sunday—a date which will certainly live in infamy on West 112th Street. The "Pearl Harbor Arch" still shows masonry left unfinished by the stonecarvers.

With great fanfare, construction resumed in 1979 under Bishop Paul Moore Jr. In the yard of the Cathedral Stoneworks, journeymen from England trained neighborhood residents as stonecutters. There was even bold talk of completing the south transept as a biosphere designed by Santiago Calatrava. But as the edifice entered its second century, the money had run out, the stoneworks was bankrupt and construction stopped again.

Completed or not, there is much to admire inside and outside this colossus. The most recent work is the main entrance, the Portal of Paradise, with figures carved from 1988 to 1997 by Simon Verity and Jean Claude Marchionni.

The Great Rose window above the entrance is the largest in the United States and contains more than 10,000 pieces of glass. The figure of Christ at the center is five feet seven inches tall. Between the window and the high altar is the longest uninterrupted vista to be found in any cathedral.

On the aisles, bays are dedicated to such pursuits as sports, history, medicine and communications. Poets' Corner, modeled on Westminster Abbey, honors American writers. The Aeolian-Skinner organ has 8,035 pipes. The sound of its state trumpet is brilliant and piercing.

Around the apse are the Chapels of the Seven Tongues, dedicated to some of the nationalities that made up New York's melting pot at the turn of the 20th century. The Chapel of St. Savior by Heins & La Farge now contains an altarpiece by Keith Haring entitled *The Life of Christ*.

Outside, the winged archangel Michael and a herd of giraffes are seen triumphant over Satan, atop the 40-foot-high Peace Fountain by Greg Wyatt (1985). Nearby is the open-air pulpit of 1916 by Howells & Stokes.

To these permanent symbols of devotion are added art exhibits, concerts, dance recitals and readings. Ecology tours explore the cycles of creation and celebrate the environment. On the first Sunday in October, St. Francis of Assisi is honored when pets and other creatures—from tarantulas to elephants—are

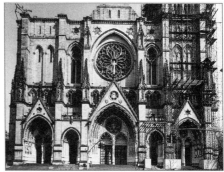

brought to the cathedral to be blessed. At other times, peacocks can be seen strutting around the grounds, known as the Close.

About St. John the Unfinished, its former dean, the Very Rev. James Parks Morton, took the long view in 1994. "Cathedrals are sort of start, stop, start, stop," he said. "They go on for hundreds of years."

The cathedral is open from 7 a.m. to 6 p.m., Monday through Saturday; 7 a.m. to 8 p.m. on Sunday. Besides Sunday morning services, there is a choral vespers and organ meditation at 7 p.m. There are also weekday Eucharist and prayer services. Tours are at 11 a.m., Tuesday through Saturday; 1 p.m. on Sunday; $3 a person. Special tours to the top of the cathedral are held on the first and third Saturday of the month at noon and 2 p.m.; $10 a person, by reservation. There is a gift shop.

Church of St. Paul and St. Andrew

263 West 86th Street,
at West End Avenue
(212) 362-3179
www.gbgm-umc.org/spsaumc

Designated landmark

A neighborhood cynosure since its completion in 1897 to designs by Robert H. Robertson, the octagonal tower of this United Methodist church is a colossal lighthouse, a spiritual beacon. It was constructed for St. Paul Church, which was joined in 1937 by the St. Andrew congregation, whose old home at 120 West 76th Street is now the West Side Institutional Synagogue.

In the 1980s, feeling terribly burdened by its oversized and deteriorating home, the congregation unsuccessfully fought landmark status. When it was denied permission in 1989 to tear down its sanctuary, the Rev. Edward C. Horne said, "The preservationists have a clear interest in preserving the building at all costs—including the congregation." Yet St. Paul and St. Andrew has endured, sharing its home with Congregation B'nai Jeshurun, Ethiopian Evangelical Mennonites and others.

Sunday service is at 11 a.m. B'nai Jeshurun holds services on Friday evenings.

West End Collegiate Church

368 West End Avenue,
at West 77th Street
(212) 787-1566
www.westendchurch.org

Designated landmark

I t took two and a half centuries of dabbling in Greek, Gothic and
Romanesque styles, but finally in 1892 the Collegiate Reformed
Protestant Dutch Church built a church that actually looked Dutch.

Not only did the architecture fit the denomination, it also fit the
setting: a pleasant area along the Hudson known to the Dutch as
Bloemendael, the "Vale of Flowers." By the 1890s, Bloomingdale was
developing rapidly enough that the consistory of the Collegiate Church

set down stakes. The architect Robert
W. Gibson drew on the cityscapes of
Amsterdam and Haarlem for inspiration, emulating the characteristically
steep roof lines and crow-step gables.
West End Collegiate also stands out
from the usual ecclesiastical gray with
its warm, yellow-orange Roman brickwork.

The West End complex included a
home for the Collegiate School, which
describes itself as the oldest independent
school in the United States, tracing its
origins to 1628, when it was established
as part of the Collegiate Church. Though the school formally separated
from church control in 1940, representatives of the consistory still serve on
its board. The Old Building on 77th Street now has classrooms for the 9th
through 12th grades, a gymnasium and a computer lab.

**Sunday worship is at 11 a.m. Child care and an infrared hearing assis-
tance system are available. Vespers are Tuesday at 6. Communion is
offered Wednesday at 8 a.m. On Tuesday, hot supper is served to the
homeless, no questions asked.**

119

Congregation Ansche Chesed
251 West 100th Street, at West End Avenue

This Byzantine Moderne complex designed by Edward I. Shire and completed in 1927 has a sanctuary that seats 1,500 and a six-story community house. Ansche Chesed (People of Mercy) is a Conservative congregation.

St. Michael's Church
225 West 99th Street, at Amsterdam Avenue

Within this Romanesque Revival sanctuary by Robert W. Gibson, completed in 1891, can be found the extraordinary suite of 22-foot-high apsidal windows by Louis Comfort Tiffany depicting St. Michael's victory in heaven.

St. Paul's Chapel
at Columbia University
near Amsterdam Avenue and West 117th Street
Designated landmark

Renaissance Revival on the outside, this splendidly compact work of 1907 by Howells & Stokes has a Byzantine interior composed almost entirely of herringboned Guastavino tiles.

Second Church of Christ, Scientist
77 Central Park West, at West 68th Street
Within a historic district

Step far back from this ornate 1900 sanctuary by Frederick R. Comstock. Its real glory is its broad copper dome, and that can only be seen at a distance.

West-Park Presbyterian Church
539 Amsterdam Avenue, at West 86th Street

A massively rugged and ruddy Romanesque Revival tower anchors this vigorous church, completed in 1890 and designed by Henry F. Kilburn to harmonize with the mid-block 1884 chapel by Leopold Eidlitz.

Upper East Side and Yorkville

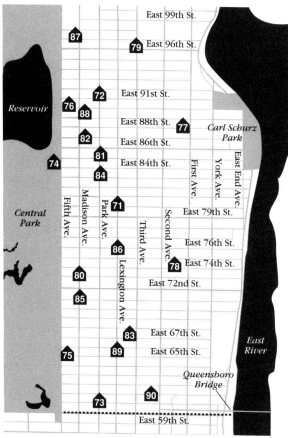

71 All Souls Church
72 Brick Presbyterian Church
73 Christ Church
74 Temple of Isis at Dendur
75 Congregation Emanu-El
76 Church of the Heavenly Rest
77 Church of the Holy Trinity
78 Greek Orthodox Cathedral of the Holy Trinity
79 Islamic Cultural Center of New York
80 Madison Avenue Presbyterian Church

81 Park Avenue Christian Church
82 Park Avenue Synagogue
83 Park East Synagogue
84 Church of St. Ignatius Loyola
85 St. James' Church
86 St. Jean Baptiste Church
87 St. Nicholas Russian Orthodox Cathedral
88 Church of St. Thomas More
89 Church of St. Vincent Ferrer
90 Trinity Baptist Church

All Souls Church

1157 Lexington Avenue,
at East 80th Street
(212) 535-5530
www.allsoulsnyc.org

Although he was descended from the great Gothic architect Richard Upjohn, and despite the fact that he was designing in the era of the Chrysler and Empire State Buildings, Hobart Upjohn reached to the Congregational meetinghouses of New England for inspiration at All Souls. He came up with a crisply detailed red-brick bell tower and steeple.

The choice was fitting, since All Souls began in 1819 as the First Congregational Church. Members of the congregation included Herman Melville; Peter Cooper, the industrialist who founded Cooper Union; Nathaniel Currier, of Currier & Ives; and William Cullen Bryant, the editor and poet.

All Souls was known as the "Church of the Holy Zebra" in the 19th century, when it occupied an exuberant Pisan sanctuary at Park Avenue South and 20th Street, designed by Jacob Wrey Mould with alternating bands of contrasting zone.

Its Lexington Avenue church opened in 1932. Now a Unitarian Universalist body, All Souls describes itself as a "congregation of open minds and hearts." It has been led for more than two decades by the Rev. F. Forrester Church, the son of Senator Frank Church of Idaho, whose charismatic style was credited with greatly revitalizing this venerable institution.

Principal services are held Sunday at 10 and 11:15 a.m. All Souls has 25 social outreach programs: Homeless Hospitality on Monday evenings; Crossing 96th Street, bringing together people from East Harlem and the Upper East Side; and an AIDS task force. It is also the home of Musica Viva, (212) 794-3646, one of the few choruses with its own orchestra, which offers programs of both sacred and secular works.

Brick Presbyterian Church

1140 Park Avenue,
at East 91st Street
(212) 289-4400
www.brickchurch.org

Within a historic district

R ich in tradition, the Brick Church has never departed far from the architecture of its first Georgian home, built while New York was ruled by the Georges. The congregation was founded in 1767 as the uptown flock of the First Presbyterian Church. Its building at Beekman Street and Park Row opened in 1768. First called the New Church, the red-brick structure was known by its more descriptive name before the end of the 18th century.

Brick moved to Fifth Avenue and 37th Street in 1858 and then to Park Avenue, building its present church from 1938 to 1940. The design, by Lewis Ayres of York & Sawyer, incorporates the bell and weather vane of the original building. The Chapel of the Reformed Faith, designed by Adams & Woodbridge, was added in 1952.

Notable members of the congregation have included John Foster Dulles, President Eisenhower's secretary of state, and Thomas J. Watson Sr., who led I.B.M. to its worldwide prominence.

Brick is highly regarded for musical programs and has a number of outlets for this form of "prayer and praise to God." The Chancel Choir, which requires an audition, sings at the 11 a.m. Sunday service and at concerts throughout the year. The Summer Choir, open to all, sings at services from Memorial Day through Labor Day. The English Handbell Ringers is an adult group open to anyone who can read music fluently. And there are four youth choirs.

Christ Church

520 Park Avenue,
at East 60th Street
(212) 838-3036
www.christchurchnyc.org

The brightest colors in a house of worship are not always found in the windows. Here they are in the vaults and arches of the ceiling—dazzling, scintillating mosaics that fracture Manhattan's monochrome and recall the fabulous tiled churches of Ravenna, Italy. Though Ralph Adams Cram was a master of Gothic, for this United Methodist sanctuary, finished in 1933, he used a robust Romanesque-Byzantine palette, explaining that the "Protestant congregation was averse to Medieval Catholicism both by inheritance and doctrine." The church, formed by the union of the Madison Avenue Methodist

Episcopal Church and the 61st Street Methodist Episcopal Church, was known around the nation during the 44-year ministry of the Rev. Ralph Washington Sockman, whose "National Radio Pulpit" was heard on NBC from 1928 to 1962.

The main service on Sunday is at 11 a.m., and there is communion in the chapel at 9 a.m. Morning prayers are on Wednesday at 7:30. The church is open Monday to Friday from 7 a.m. to 6 p.m. and 11 a.m. to 3 p.m. on Saturday. Guided tours are available on the third Sunday of every month after the 11 a.m. service, or by arrangement.

Temple of Isis at Dendur

Metropolitan Museum of Art
1000 Fifth Avenue,
at East 82nd Street
(212) 535-7710
www.metmuseum.org

The only house of worship in Manhattan built during the reign of Caesar Augustus sits on its own serene island, overlooking Central Park from behind a cool, vast wall of glass. The setting in the Sackler Wing of the Metropolitan Museum is one of exotic mystery at night; by day, surpassing tranquillity.

But the story of the temple is pure tumult—from its very origins more than 2,000 years ago in the Nubian settlement of Dendur in Upper Egypt. During a battle with Abyssinia, Petesi and Pihor, the sons of a local chieftain, were drowned in the Nile. This shrine, dedicated to their memory and to the goddess Isis, was built around 15 B.C. by order of Emperor Augustus. Reliefs carved into its sandstone walls depict Isis, Osiris, Horus and Augustus himself, dressed as pharaoh. In 577 the temple was converted into a Coptic church.

In the early 1960s, as the Aswan High Dam was being built, the waters of the Nile in Upper Egypt began rising to create Lake Nasser. Dendur was one of the ancient sites threatened with inundation, along with the colossal temple of Abu Simbel, which was relocated with financial assistance from the United States. Grateful for that aid, the Egyptian government offered the smaller temple to America in 1965.

The Met and the Smithsonian vied for this extraordinary archeological prize, and were joined in the tussle by 20 other cities, including Cairo, Illinois. In 1968, 660 stones composing the temple were loaded aboard a freighter for the journey to America, along with Italian cheeses, canned tomatoes and maraschino cherries.

Even after New York won the temple, the battle continued, as the Met's expansion plans were strenuously opposed on the grounds that

the Sackler Wing, designed by Kevin Roche John Dinkeloo Associates, would devour precious acreage in Central Park. But in 1978 the addition was finally opened and the temple began receiving visitors again.

The Museum is open every day but Monday. The suggested admission is $10 for adults, $5 for students and the elderly.

Congregation Emanu-El

1 East 65th Street,
at Fifth Avenue
(212) 744-1400
www.emanuelnyc.org

Within a historic district

Superlatives abound at Temple Emanu-El: the largest synagogue in the world is home to the largest Reform congregation in the nation—10,000 people—and the oldest Reform congregation in the city, founded in 1845 to serve the growing number of German Jews.

Begun with 33 members in rented space at Grand and Clinton Streets, Emanu-El (God Is With Us) moved to Chrystie Street in 1848, then to the Twelfth Street Baptist Church in 1854. That building, 120 East 12th Street, still stands and is now St. Ann's Armenian Catholic Church. Emanu-El moved in 1868 to a grand Moorish sanctuary at Fifth Avenue and 43rd Street, designed by Leopold Eidlitz. It was here that the first permanent English-speaking rabbi, Gustave Gottheil, was installed. (For most of the 20th century, Emanu-El had only two senior rabbis: Nathan A. Perilman and Ronald B. Sobel. Its longtime cantor, Howard Nevison, was the first cantor to sing at the Vatican.)

In 1927, under the leadership of Louis Marshall, Emanu-El merged with Congregation Beth El (House of God), at Fifth Avenue and 76th Street, and began constructing the enormous 65th Street sanctuary. It was designed by Robert D. Kohn, Charles Butler and Clarence Stein, who described the architecture as "Romanesque as used in the south of Italy under the influence of the Moorish, because it was an expression of the intermingling of Occidental and Oriental thought." The stained-glass windows were made by Oliver Smith and

the Nicola D'Ascenzo Studio. Tiffany windows from the 43rd Street building were also brought here. The temple opened in 1929.

The soaring, dimly mysterious main sanctuary, which seats 2,500, has walls that seem to be threaded with lambent strands of light. It is well suited in its quiet majesty for memorial services. Some of the most prominent Americans have been eulogized here, including William Paley, Iphigene Ochs Sulzberger and Theodore White. It has even been claimed in advance by the very much living. Mayor Edward I. Koch said in 1987 that he planned for his funeral to be here. Asked why, he replied, "Oh, because I want to have a large synagogue."

The synagogue is open every day from 10 a.m. to 5 p.m. for meditation, prayer and rest. There are services every day at 5:30 p.m., and Sabbath services with music at 5:15 p.m. on Friday and 10:30 a.m. Saturday. The Friday service is broadcast on WQXR, 96.3 FM. Tours are available Sunday through Friday and beginning at noon on Saturday. The Judaica Collection contains nearly 500 art objects and historic memorabilia. There is a nursery school, a religious school and continuing education for adults. Film, lecture and music programs are offered throughout the year, including the Ecumenical Concert on the first Sunday in May, when choirs from neighboring churches sing with the synagogue's.

Church of the Heavenly Rest

2 East 90th Street,
at Fifth Avenue
(212) 289-3400
www.heavenlyrest.org

Within a historic district

Heavenly rest was what the veterans of the Civil War were hoping for when they formed this parish in 1865. Their first church was at Fifth Avenue and 45th Street. Under the Rev. Henry Darlington, the congregation merged with the Church of the Beloved Disciple and acquired this site from Andrew Carnegie's widow, Louise, who lived across the street. To protect the view out her window, she stipulated a 75-foot height limit. But the resulting church was in no way diminished. This muscular limestone mesa, finished in 1929, was designed by Mayers, Murray & Philip, with sculptures by Lee Lawrie and Malvina Hoffman. During a restoration, it suffered a devastating fire in August 1993. The stained-glass windows were spared, the Rev. C. Hugh Hildesley said gratefully, because firefighters carefully and deliberately used more complicated means to ventilate the 1,000-degree blaze.

Rebounding, the church expanded the restoration project, designed by Gerald Allen and Jeffrey Harbinson.

There are services on Sunday at 8 and 10:30 a.m., plus an education hour for all ages at 9:30. Wednesday services are at noon and 6:30 p.m. It is home to the Canterbury Choral Society, a 100-voice chorus that specializes in oratorio, the New York Pro Arte Chamber Orchestra, and a series called Heavenly Jazz.

Church of the Holy Trinity

312 East 88th Street,
near First Avenue
(212) 289-4100
www.holytrinity-nyc.org

Designated landmark

Almost a proto-Woolworth Building, the bell tower at the Episcopal Church of the Holy Trinity presages the skyscraper era with its thrillingly vertical rendering of Gothic. Adding to its appeal is the setting: a quarter-acre of sweetly landscaped grounds, on which are also set St. Christopher House and a parsonage.

Serena Rhinelander gets the credit for this verdant little complex, built from 1895 to 1899, which occupies a site that was once part of her family's estate. Desirous of seeing a church surrounded by grass and trees in the working-class neighborhood, she offered to build this mission for St. James' parish.

The architects, Barney & Chapman, designed another inner-city mission campus for the Episcopal church on East 14th Street that is now the Immaculate Conception Roman Catholic Church.

Holy Trinity became an independent parish in 1951. The bells were restored in 1995 under the direction of the conservator William Stivale.

Sunday worship services are at 8, 9 and 11 a.m. and 6 p.m. The church is open to visitors throughout the day. It has a thrift shop that is open on Saturday. The 60-rank Rieger pipe organ that was installed in 1988 attracts organists from around the world to play recitals. The church also sponsors a large number of music, theater and dance programs.

Greek Orthodox Cathedral of the Holy Trinity

319 East 74th Street,
near Second Avenue
(212) 288-3215
www.thecathedral.goarch.org

A cathedral is where the bishop sits. It is not necessarily the largest church in town. There are a dozen cathedrals in Manhattan besides St. Patrick's and St. John the Divine, and this mid-block Byzantine Moderne struc-
ture is one of the most important. It is the seat of the largest Orthodox Christian church in the United States: the Greek Orthodox Archdiocese of America, with 1.5 million members. The archdiocese was led from 1959 to 1996 by Archbishop Iakovos, the first Orthodox leader to meet with a Pope in 350 years. Iakovos also marched with the Rev. Martin Luther King Jr. in Selma in 1965.

Though the faith goes back a millennium, the Greek Orthodox presence is relatively new in New York. In 1892 Holy Trinity Church rented space in what is now St. Benedict Roman Catholic Church, at 340 West 53rd Street. Its present sanctuary, by Kerr Rainsford, John A. Thompson and Gerald A. Holmes, was built from 1931 to 1932 and was designated a cathedral in 1962. The dean of the cathedral for many years has been the Rev. Robert G. Stephanopoulos, whose son George was an adviser to President Clinton and a political commentator.

The cathedral has witnessed solemn moments, like the visit in 1990 of Demetrios I, the first Ecumenical Patriarch to travel to the United States. And it has seen trying moments, including the turmoil leading to the resignation in 1999 of Archbishop Spyridon, whose critics questioned his ruling style and his handling of educational and financial matters. Spyridon was succeeded by Archbishop Demetrios, who received the staff symbolizing his elevation from former Archbishop Iakovos himself.

The cathedral holds one service every Sunday, from 9:30 a.m. to noon. The building is closed at other times, but anyone wishing to visit may enter through the office at 337 East 74th Street.

129

Islamic Cultural Center of New York

1711 Third Avenue,
at East 96th Street
(212) 722-5234
salam.muslimsonline.com/~iccny

Visitors to this prayer hall must leave behind three things. Two are their shoes; the third is any preconception of what a mosque "should" look like. Here there are no richly colored tiles or keyhole-shaped arches. (In New York, that Moorish touch is reserved for synagogues.) Instead, this is a spare, serene, modernist work by Skidmore, Owings & Merrill, built from 1987 to 1991. The minaret is by Swanke Hayden Connell.

The mosque is skewed 29 degrees off the Manhattan street grid, oriented toward the Kaaba shrine in the Grand Mosque of Mecca, the most sacred place of Islam. That direction is indicated by the points of the crescent moons atop the dome and minaret, and by a niche called the mihrab.

Simplicity stripped the design of national attributes, a vital consideration for a project that, though funded largely by Kuwaitis, depended on support from many Islamic countries. Simplicity also encourages meditation. One need not be steeped in the Koran to appreciate the sanctity of this luminous space, where a diaphanous cylinder of 90 bulbs hanging by brass rods from the drum of the dome resembles the low-slung oil lamps of Hagia Sophia. Other Islamic elements include stylized calligraphic ornaments, a separate women's gallery and a minbar, the staircase topped by a pulpit from which the imam preaches.

The mosque briefly took center stage in civic life in 1999, when it was the setting of a memorial service for Amadou Diallo, a West African street vendor whose killing by the police brought a firestorm of criticism upon the administration of Mayor Rudolph W. Giuliani.

Friday prayers, or jumu'ah, are at 12:30 p.m. from October to April, 1 p.m. from April to October. Visitors can go to the ground-floor office on 97th Street between 10 a.m. and 4 p.m., except Friday afternoons during the main prayer service. Groups should call for an appointment. Casual or revealing clothes should not be worn, and women should be prepared to cover their heads.

Madison Avenue Presbyterian Church

921 Madison Avenue,
at East 73rd Street
(212) 288-8920
www.mapc.com

Within a historic district

With a tower that would not be out of place in King Ludwig's Neuschwanstein Castle, and a nine-story Church House by James Gamble Rogers that overshadows the tower, the Madison Avenue Presbyterian Church cuts a high profile.

Appropriately, some of the most powerful and influential names in New York City history are associated with this church, beginning with James Lenox—of the Lenox Hill Lenoxes—who gave this site to the Phillips Presbyterian Church, named in honor of the Rev. William Wirt Phillips. The Phillips congregation merged in 1899 with the Madison Avenue Presbyterian Chuch and built this Gothic sanctuary by James E. Ware & Son. (Part of an earlier church on this site, built in 1869, survives as the Phillips Chapel.)

Other leading figures here have included the Rev. Henry Sloane Coffin, who was pastor from 1905 to 1926 (his nephew, the Rev. William Sloane Coffin Jr., was senior minister at Riverside Church); Edward S. Harkness, Henry Coffin's roommate at Yale and a Standard Oil heir; and Henry R. Luce, the founder of Time Inc. and son of a Presbyterian missionary, who was a parishioner.

During a renovation begun in 1998 by the Rev. Fred R. Anderson, the architect Page Ayres Cowley of Cowley & Prudon discovered lovely oak triforium screens with St. Andrew's crosses under plywood panels that had been installed in a 1961 remodeling. The screens were gloriously restored.

Sunday services are at 9 and 11:15 a.m. On the first Wednesday of the month is a Healing and Wholeness Communion Service at 6 p.m. Since 1973 the Saint Andrew Music Society has conducted concerts every Sunday at 4 p.m., from October to May.

Park Avenue Christian Church

1010 Park Avenue,
at East 85th Street
(212) 288-3246
e-mail: paccnyc@aol.com

Abruptly vertical, this Gothic church has been compared to the Sainte-Chapelle in Paris because of its proportions and its slender 70-foot spire, known as a fleche. Built from 1909 to 1911, it was designed by Cram, Goodhue & Ferguson, and foreshadows Bertram Grosvenor Goodhue's Church of the Intercession in upper Manhattan. The main window is by Louis Comfort Tiffany. An inscription on the façade, "Een Drach Maakt Macht" ("In Unity There Is Strength"), is a reminder that the church was built for a Dutch Reformed congregation, the New South Church, founded in 1693. The building was later used by the Park Avenue Presbyterian Church before being taken over by the Christian Church (Disciples of Christ) denomination, which undertook a renovation in 1990. Music plays a large part in the life of this church, which is known for its Easter and Christmas programs.

The Sunday service is at 11 a.m. A midweek vesper service is usually on the second Wednesday of the month. An ecumenical dance choir teaches techniques of sacred dance as part of the worship.

Park Avenue Synagogue

50 East 87th Street,
at Madison Avenue
(212) 369-2600

When you first approach this impressive complex, you're neither on Park Avenue nor are you looking at a synagogue. Instead, what you see is a five-story classroom and auditorium building, with tall arched bays wrapping around the corner of 87th Street and Madison Avenue. Designed by James Rush Jarrett with Schuman Lichtenstein Claman & Efron, it was built in 1980 to memorialize the one million Jewish children who perished in the Holocaust.

The mid-block synagogue itself was built in 1927 and designed by Walter S. Schneider with the same kind of monumental, recessed central portal he used at the earlier B'nai Jeshurun. This façade is more elaborately faceted, with strip pilasters framing the arch, over which is the inscription "I love your temple abode, the dwelling-place of your glory" (Psalms 26).

A 1955 annex by Kelly & Gruzen, with a stained-glass façade by Adolf Gottlieb, was named for the renowned Rabbi Milton Steinberg, author of *The Making of the Modern Jew* and *As a Driven Leaf*. It was subsumed by the 1980 addition.

This Conservative congregation, long known for its distinguished members and its commitment to the arts, is descended from Beth Israel (House of Israel), which merged with Bikur Cholim (Visitors to the Sick) and then with Agudat Yesharim (Group of the Righteous), a name still in use today. As for how it came to be called the Park Avenue Synagogue, Rabbi David H. Lincoln thinks that it may simply have sounded better than "Madison Avenue Synagogue."

This large, active congregation offers services beginning at 6:15 p.m. Friday, resuming at 7:30 a.m. Saturday. There are services at 7:15 a.m., Monday through Friday, and 4:45 p.m., Sunday through Thursday. Once each spring and fall it holds "concert services," at which a cantor and choir introduce previously unheard choral works.

133

Park East Synagogue

163 East 67th Street,
near Third Avenue
(212) 737-6900

Designated landmark

There are few other flights of architectural fancy on this scale in New York. Moorish, Byzantine and Romanesque, it is an astonishing, almost hallucinatory, presence with dozens of arches and apertures in ample horseshoe shapes, sinuous ogees and delicate multifoils. The towers flanking the rose window are asymmetrical, adding to the picturesque quality. There are grand stairs and granite plaques, one of which declares: "Enter into His gates with Thanksgiving and into His courts with praise" (Psalms 100).

Congregation Zichron Ephraim literally means a "memorial to Ephraim"—Ephraim Weil—from his sons Jonas and Samuel, who gave the land and money for this building. In 1887, after Rabbi Bernard Drachman resigned from Beth Israel Bikur Cholim when that congregation resolved to seat men and women together, Jonas Weil, a real estate investor, proposed the establishment of a new synagogue that would represent a "harmonious combination of Orthodox Judaism and Americanism." Designed by Ernst Schneider and Henry Herter, it was finished in 1890.

Zichron Ephraim, which has long emphasized education (Harry Houdini was in its first Talmud Torah class), operates a day school and cultural center at 164 East 68th Street. Rabbi Arthur Schneier, who survived the death camps during the Holocaust, arrived at Park East in 1962 and soon thereafter established the the Appeal of Conscience Foundation to support religious freedom. An exterior

restoration, designed by the architectural firm Dan Peter Kopple & Associates, was completed in 1997.

Candle lighting is at sundown on Friday and Saturday services begin at 9 a.m. There is a Sephardic service every Saturday morning, usually at 9:15. Daily services are at 7:45 a.m. and at 9 a.m. on Sunday.

134

Church of
St. Ignatius Loyola

980 Park Avenue,
at East 84th Street
(212) 288-3588
www.saintignatiusloyola.org

Designated landmark

In 1994 the eyes of the world were focused on this lusciously Baroque, Jesuit-run Roman Catholic church. The occasion was the funeral of Jacqueline Kennedy Onassis, who was christened here 64 years earlier. It says much about the prominence of this parish that it played a central role at the beginning and the end of the life of one of New York's First Citizens.

It also says much about the parish and its high regard for liturgical art that in 1993 it installed the largest mechanical-action organ in New York: a 68-stop, 5,000-pipe instrument, with four keyboards (manuals), by N.P. Mander Ltd. of London. Kent Tritle, the music director here, is principal organist of the American Symphony Orchestra.

The parish, founded in 1851, was originally dedicated to St. Lawrence O'Toole before being entrusted to the Society of Jesus in 1866. In 1884 it began a Gothic Revival church on this site. That project was abandoned, but the basement story is evident on 84th Street and forms Wallace Hall, formerly the St. Lawrence O'Toole chapel. The basilica-like upper sanctuary, by Schickel & Ditmars, was dedicated in 1898. The ceiling of the nave is a gilt, coffered barrel vault supported by pink granite columns. The façade recalls Il Gesù, the Jesuits' mother church in Rome, and is inscribed with the society's motto: "To the Greater Glory of God."

The church is open only for Masses or special events, such as concerts. There are weekday Masses at 8:30 a.m., 12:10 and 5:30 p.m. The Saturday vigil is at 5:30 p.m. Sunday Masses are at 7:30, 9:30 and 11 a.m., 12:30 and 7:30 p.m. For information about the concert series, Sacred Music in a Sacred Space, call (212) 288-2520. A Mander organ representative will demonstrate the instrument on request. Call (203) 348-8085.

St. James' Church

A three-dimensional lesson in architectural history, St. James' Church looks like the patchwork amalgam it is: the bones of a robust 1884 Romanesque design by R. H. Robertson, reoriented and reclad with a Gothic overlay by Ralph Adams Cram in 1924, then topped with an anemic steeple by Richard A. Kimball in 1950.

Far lovelier inside than outside, the church was ornamented with a great rose window and a carved altar screen, or reredos, in the 1920s. Under the Rev. Brenda G. Husson, a plan for the renovation of the church and parish house was drawn up in 1999 by the architect Lee Harris Pomeroy.

St. James' is one of New York's foremost Episcopal congregations, though it began modestly in 1810 as a country chapel for an East River summer colony known as Hamilton Square, sharing its rector with St. Michael's, on the other side of Manhattan. The second St. James' church, by James Renwick Jr., stood on East 72nd Street, near Third Avenue.

The Rev. Horace W. B. Donegan, rector from 1933 to 1947, went on to become bishop of the New York diocese. In 1951 St. James' mission chapel on East 88th Street, Holy Trinity, became an independent parish.

The church is open every day from 8 a.m. to 7 p.m. Sunday services are at 8, 9:15 and 11:15 a.m. and 6 p.m. Holy Eucharist is also celebrated on Tuesday at 7:30 a.m., Wednesday at 8 a.m. and 6 p.m. and Thursday at 12:05 p.m. There are active adult education, youth and family programs.

St. Jean Baptiste Church

1067 Lexington Avenue,
at East 76th Street
(212) 288-5082
www.sjbrcc.org

Designated landmark

Though this twin-towered church could nobly crown the Spanish Steps in Rome, it is descended from humble roots: the "Crib of Bethlehem," as the first home of the Roman Catholic parish was called. When the French Canadians of Yorkville joined to worship in 1882, they had to use a stable at 202 East 77th Street, which still stands, suffering the noise and smells from below. They did much better with their next home, designed by Napoleon Le Brun, at 159 East 76th Street.

The present Renaissance-style monument, by Nicholas Serracino, was built from 1912 to 1914. It is notable for its 175-foot-high dome, for its stained-glass windows by the Lorin studio of Chartres, and for the fact that the cost was borne by one man, Thomas Fortune Ryan, the financier and street-railway monopolist.

Since 1900 the church has been in the care of the Congregation of the Most Blessed Sacrament. Under the Rev. John A. Kamas, the church undertook a $6 million renovation in the 1990s, made possible by the sale of its air rights to the developer of the Siena apartment tower to the east. The once somber interior was redecorated by Felix Chavez with vivid colors that were meant in part to play off the newly vibrant Lorin windows, restored by Patrick Clark.

St. Jean maintains a vigorous devotion schedule, with six Sunday Masses, morning and evening prayer services daily, holy hours, benedictions, novenas, prayer meetings and rosary recitations. Its musical offerings include three concerts a year by the Amor Artis Chorus and Orchestra.

137

St. Nicholas Russian Orthodox Cathedral

15 East 97th Street,
near Madison Avenue
(212) 289-1915
www.stnicholasronyc.com

Designated landmark

Built, as the cornerstone says, in the reign of the "Most Pious Autocrat and Great Emperor Nicholas Alexandrovich of All Russias" (Czar Nicholas II), this cathedral is dedicated to St. Nicholas the Wonder-worker. And its exuberant riot of colorful Muscovite Baroque design—especially the five great onion domes—inspires wonder to this day.

The cathedral's story is as dramatic as the setting. The Rev. Alexander Hotovitzky of Kremenets, Ukraine, came to the fledgling St. Nicholas parish, at Second Avenue and 19th Street, in 1895. To raise money for a new church, Hotovitzky traveled to Russia in 1900, having secured imperial permission to solicit funds throughout the empire. The first donation of 5,000 rubles came from the Czar himself.

St. Nicholas Church was built from 1901 to 1902 and designed by I. V. Bergessen, a Russian architect. With all of its lavish details, the only thing that seemed to be missing—to Western eyes—were the pews. But here, worshipers stand during services.

The American See of the Russian church was transferred to New York in 1905, and St. Nicholas became the cathedral. Hotovitzky was the dean until 1914, when he returned to Russia, where he died in a concentration camp in 1937. He was canonized in 1994.

Following the Russian Revolution, a struggle began for the cathedral in 1923, when the Rev. John Kedrovsky was appointed Metropolitan for North and South America by the schismatic, Soviet-controlled Living Church in Moscow. Church leaders in America refused to recognize him because of the Bolshevik taint of his credentials. The battle between them involved "raids, riots, court injunctions and the wielding of axes against the church doors," *The New York Times* reported. American

courts recognized Kedrovsky as the claimant in 1925. Another battle erupted in 1945, when an American-based Metropolitanate (Russian Orthodox diocese) was briefly awarded control by the courts under a law that sought to eliminate Communist influence in state-chartered Russian Orthodox churches. The law was overturned by the Supreme Court in 1952.

Today the cathedral is the seat of Bishop Mercurius, head of the parishes belonging to the Moscow Patriarchate of the Russian Orthodox Church in the U.S.A.

Divine liturgy with a professional choir is conducted on Sunday at 10 a.m. in Slavonic, with some English. There is a vesper service on Saturday at 6 p.m. The cathedral is closed at other times, but visitors may ring the office bell between 9 a.m. and 5 p.m.

Church of
St. Thomas More

59 East 89th Street,
near Madison Avenue
(212) 876-7718

L ike Christ & St. Stephen's across town, this building has the picturesque air of a country Gothic church. And that is exactly what it was in 1870. When the Episcopal church of St. Luke in the Fields moved its Home for Indigent Christian Females from Greenwich Village to the distant suburbs around East 89th Street, the residents needed a place of worship. The philanthropist Caroline Talman financed this sanctuary, known originally as the Church of the Beloved Disciple. It was designed by Hubert & Pirsson, architects of the Chelsea Hotel.

The parish merged in the 1920s with the nearby Church of the Heavenly Rest, which still maintains a Beloved Disciple chapel. (That nameless disciple is usually said to be John.)

After serving as the East 89th Street Reformed Church, this sanctuary became a Roman Catholic church in 1950, named for Sir Thomas More, the "man for all seasons" and lord chancellor of England who was executed in 1535 for refusing to recognize King

Henry VIII as head of the English church.

Tranquil and venerable, St. Thomas More was a little-known local treasure until 1999, when it fell into the international spotlight as the setting of a memorial Mass for John F. Kennedy Jr., whose mother had been a parishioner here.

Sunday Masses are at 8, 10 and 11:15 a.m., 12:30, 5:45 and 7:30 p.m. Daily Masses are at 7 (except Saturday) and 8 a.m., 12:15 and 5:45 p.m. At other times, one can enter the church through the rectory.

Church of
St. Vincent Ferrer

881 Lexington Avenue,
at East 66th Street
(212) 744-2080
www.fordham.edu/halsall/
medny/mchale.html

Designated landmark

An ancient architectural vernacular is swept here into the industrial age with pistonlike buttresses framing deep aisle windows, the whole bearing forward with a splendid thrust, not unlike a great ecclesiastical locomotive.

St. Vincent Ferrer, built from 1916 to 1918, is unmistakably the work of Bertram Grosvenor Goodhue, whose innovations still feel so freshly powerful that one is tempted to rank him ahead of Richard Upjohn, James Renwick and perhaps even Ralph Adams Cram as America's master Gothicist. Goodhue   considered St. Vincent Ferrer his best church.

This Roman Catholic parish is run by the Dominicans, or Order of Preachers (O.P.), who founded it in 1867. They chose Goodhue for this church in part because of his work at St. Thomas on Fifth Avenue. Lee Lawrie, sculptor of the famous St. Thomas reredos, was once again the ideal collaborator. And the cobalt of Charles Connick's glass is so rich that it appears almost too deep to admit light.

There are four Masses every day: at 8 a.m., 9 a.m. (10 on Sunday), 12:10 (noon on Sunday, with choir) and 5:30 p.m. The church remains open between services, until 6:15 p.m.

Trinity Baptist Church

250 East 61st Street,
near Second Avenue
(212) 838-6844
www.tbcny.org

Within a historic district

Could this be a church? Your eye is caught by a stepped, planar, abstract façade in graduated colors of brick, ranging from loamy brown to bright marigold. You are transported to Stockholm between the World Wars. The Scandinavian sensibility continues within: blond woods, bottle-blue glass, bold geometry and expressionistic ornament.

If you doubt that Art Deco exuberance could be put to liturgical purpose, you'll leave wishing there were more buildings like this little gem. But it is sui generis by design; the specialized work of a Swedish architect, Martin Gravely Hedmark, for a congregation known as the First Swedish Baptist Church at the time this sanctuary was built, from 1929 to 1931. Hedmark created a sampler of native motifs, with two bell towers modeled on originals in Stockholm, flanking a gabled roof whose stepped profile recalls buildings along the Baltic. A restoration project began in 1991, under the conservator William Stivale.

The Baptist congregation, founded in 1867, conducted its major services in Swedish until 1942, when English was adopted, along with a new name, Trinity Baptist, reflecting the diminishing Swedish population. By 1977 there were only 58 members. But new pastors helped turn the church around and one of New York's most unusual sanctuaries is now the spiritual home of more than 330 people.

Sunday services at this popular church are at 9 and 10:45 a.m., with refreshments after each (first-timers are urged to use a red cup, so as to be identified and welcomed), and at 12:30 p.m. There is a prayer service on Wednesday at 7 p.m.

First Hungarian Reformed Church
346 East 69th Street, near First Avenue

In 1916, before his name became synonymous with luxury apartment houses and utilitarian office towers, Emery Roth designed this charming mid-block sanctuary, mixing Vienna Secessionist motifs with the vernacular style of his native Hungary.

Church of Our Lady of Good Counsel
236 East 90th Street, near Second Avenue

The architect Thomas F. Poole made stone look like lacework at St. Thomas the Apostle uptown. Here is another Roman Catholic church with the same delicate Gothic quality and by the same hand, completed in 1892.

Church of St. Catherine of Siena
411 East 68th Street, near First Avenue

A rare example of Arts and Crafts style in a New York church, this Roman Catholic sanctuary was built in 1931 and designed by Wilfred E. Anthony. Go inside. The surprise of it—springing, pointed arches sweeping over the nave—must be seen.

Third Church of Christ, Scientist
585 Park Avenue, at East 63rd Street

A refined red-brick and limestone Georgian meetinghouse on a large scale, designed by Delano & Aldrich and completed in 1924.

Harlem, El Barrio and Upper Manhattan

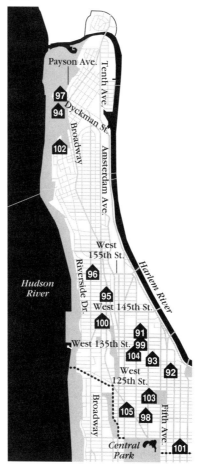

91 Abyssinian Baptist Church
92 All Saints Church
93 Bethel A. M. E. Church
94 The Cloisters
95 Church of the Crucifixion
96 Church of the Intercession
97 Church of Jesus Christ of Latter-day Saints
98 Masjid Malcolm Shabazz
99 Mother A. M. E. Zion Church
100 Church of Our Lady of Lourdes
101 St. Cecilia's Church
102 Shrine of St. Frances Xavier Cabrini
103 St. Martin's Church
104 St. Philip's Church
105 Church of St. Thomas the Apostle

Abyssinian Baptist Church

132 Odell M. Clark Place (West 138th Street),
near Adam Clayton Powell Jr. Boulevard
(212) 862-7474
www.adcorp.org/abyssinianchurch.html

Designated landmark

Looking for a place to worship, several traders visiting from Abyssinia (now Ethiopia) arrived at the First Baptist Church on Gold Street one Sunday in 1808. But they were ushered to the slave loft. "Wealthy, educated world travelers, proud human beings, with a well-defined philosophy of religion that matched that of anyone in that auditorium, they resented this and walked out in protest," the Rev. Adam Clayton Powell Jr. wrote many years later. Eighteen black members of First Baptist joined their boycott, forming the nucleus of Abyssinian, which was founded on Worth Street.

Abyssinian moved to Waverly Place in 1856, when Greenwich Village was an African-American hub, then followed the black population uptown, to West 40th Street. Its minister, the Rev. Adam Clayton Powell Sr., a champion of equal rights whose parents had been slaves, finally moved the church to West 138th Street (now named Odell M. Clark Place, after a longtime deacon).

Its present home was built from 1922 to 1923 and designed by Charles W. Bolton & Son in Tudor Gothic style, faced in bluestone, with two towers flanking an enormous window. Its distinctive floor plan has radiating seats like those in an amphitheater.

The younger Powell assumed the pulpit in 1937, and in 1944 became the first African-American elected to the House of Representatives from New York State. He was described in his *New York Times* obituary as the "leader of the largest church congregation in the nation, a political demagogue, a Congressional rebel, a civil rights leader three decades before the Montgomery bus boycott, a wheeler-dealer, a rabble-rouser, a grandstander, a fugitive, a playboy and a most effective chairman of the House Committee on Education and Labor."

Powell was followed by the Rev. Samuel DeWitt Proctor, a more scholarly and less political figure, who was succeeded in turn by the charismatic Rev. Calvin O. Butts III, who used the Abyssinian pulpit to speak out against police brutality, economic inequality and the manipulation of black consumers by tobacco and alcohol companies.

On its own and through the Abyssinian Development Corporation, established by Butts in 1989, the church has been involved in creating 800 units of housing, including Abyssinian Towers for the elderly and Abyssinian House for homeless families; 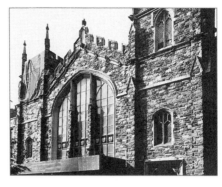 in establishing the Thurgood Marshall Academy for Learning and Social Change, a school for 500 students in grades 6 through 12; assisting low-income families; and developing commercial projects such as Harlem's first full-service supermarket in decades, a Pathmark on East 125th Street, and Harlem Center, a retail and commercial complex planned for West 125th Street.

The renowned gospel choir sings at the 9 and 11 a.m. Sunday services, making them so popular that the church asks to be notified if groups of 10 or more plan to attend. Tours were suspended in 1996, when a large-scale restoration began, but are expected to resume once it is complete.

All Saints Church

Out of a neighbor-hood whose houses of worship tend toward small scale and modest understatement erupts this magificent, effusive Venetian Gothic mountain range, completed in 1893. Besides its sheer size—almost a block long—All Saints is notable for the extremely unusual wheel windows in the clerestory, the intricately patterned and robustly colorful brickwork and the sheer drama of its craggy piers and buttresses. Its tall, slender bell tower is a neighborhood cynosure.

This Roman Catholic parish was founded in 1879. To design the sanctuary, it commissioned Renwick, Aspinwall & Russell, successors to James Renwick Jr., the architect of St. Patrick's Cathedral. Today the parish is predominantly African-American. Twice a month, it offers an Igbo Mass, celebrated as in Nigeria, where it originated among the Igbo (or Ibo) people.

Mass on Sunday is at 10 a.m. with a gospel choir; Monday through Friday at 7 a.m. Visitors at other times should enter through the rectory. The Igbo Mass is celebrated at 4:30 p.m. on the second and fourth Sunday of each month.

Bethel A.M.E. Church

60 West 132nd Street,
near Malcolm X Boulevard
(212) 862-0100

"Taught by the Declaration of Independence, sustained by the Constitution of the United States, this nation can no more resist the advancing tread of the hosts of the oncoming blacks than it can bind the stars or halt the resistless motion of the tide." So said the Rev. Reverdy C. Ransom, pastor of Bethel African Methodist Church in the early 20th century, bishop in the denomination and an organizer of the Niagara Movement, forerunner of the N.A.A.C.P.

Founded on Mott Street in 1819, Bethel moved to Second Street and then to West 25th Street. Even in the 1840s, though, it was already ministering to a small black population in the faraway town of Harlem. It was also a stop on the Underground Railroad. The 25th Street church was in the middle of the notorious Tenderloin district, which Ransom deplored as a "valley of Baca," devoid of spiritual waters and filled with "moral shipwrecks" and "ravening wolves."

In 1912 Bethel joined the exodus to Harlem, building a sanctuary designed by Wengenroth & Matsin that rather resembles a Gothic proscenium arch for the enormous central window. Members of Bethel have included A. Philip Randolph, founder of the Brotherhood of Sleeping Car Porters, and Roy Wilkins, executive director of the N.A.A.C.P. It was here in 1917 that Marcus Garvey was offered a platform to expound on his Back-to-Africa movement. Soon thereafter, he founded the Universal Negro Improvement Association.

More recent visitors included President Clinton in 1994 and Hillary Rodham Clinton in 2000, during her campaign for the Senate.

There are two services every Sunday, at 7 and 11 a.m., with full choirs. Group tours and visitors are welcome but should call ahead.

The Cloisters

Fort Tryon Park
(212) 923-3700
www.metmuseum.org

Designated landmark

Standing triumphantly atop the forces of evil, Saint Martin gazes down serenely from the apse as he has for eight and a half centuries, ever since the Romanesque church of San Martín was built on a hillside in the village of Fuentidueña, about 100 miles north of Madrid. To see him—and Daniel in the lion's den, plus assorted centaurs, serpents and sirens—no passport is needed. Just a Metrocard to get aboard the A train to 190th Street. (The same trip brings you conveniently to the Shrine of St. Frances Xavier Cabrini, too.)

Opened in 1938, the Cloisters was a gift to the Metropolitan Museum of Art from John D. Rockefeller Jr. It was designed by Allen, Collens & Willis—architects of Riverside Church, another Rockefeller benefaction overlooking the Hudson—to incorporate medieval sculpture and architecture.

But the Fuentidueña Chapel was not originally included. It took more than 20 years of negotiation, interrupted by war, before the Spanish government agreed in 1957 to lend indefinitely the beautiful surviving apse of the San Martín church, which was otherwise a ruin. In an operation prefiguring the relocation of the Temple of Dendur, the apse was dismantled into 3,300 stones, shipped to America, re-erected and opened in 1961.

To appreciate its architectural integrity, be sure to walk out to the far end of the west terrace, where a small doorway affords a fine view of the exterior.

Another 12th-century church incorporated into the Cloisters is the Langon Chapel, which includes architectural remnants of the choir

and chapel of Nôtre-Dame-du-Bourg, built around 1155 in Langon, near Bordeaux. Chapel lore suggests that the column capital with two crowned heads represents Eleanor of Aquitaine and her husband, King Henry II of England, who once visited the monastery with which the Langon church was associated. This would have been about 775 years before the A train began running.

The Cloisters are open every day but Monday. The suggested admission is $10 for adults, $5 for students and the elderly.

Church of the Crucifixion

459 West 149th Street,
at Convent Avenue
(212) 281-0900

Corbusier comes to Harlem? Well, no, but this Episcopal church, designed by Costas Machlouzarides in 1967, comes as close as anything in Manhattan to Le Corbusier's Nôtre-Dame-du-Haut in Ronchamp, France. (Machlouzarides also designed the Calhoun School Learning Center, resembling a giant television set, at West End Avenue and 81st Street.) The Crucifixion parish, founded in 1916, had occupied the former Hamilton Grange Reformed Church on the site, which was destroyed in a 1963 fire. This concrete church was built on its foundations, with each curving section holding a different function: altar, baptistry, chapel and shrine. Light is admitted through clerestory windows. Like the Civic Center Synagogue, Crucifixion reflects an attempt in the 1960s to find new expressive forms for religious sanctuaries.

Sunday Mass is at 10:15 a.m. On Tuesday through Friday, between 9:30 a.m. and 4 p.m., those wishing to visit may ring the upper bell at the office.

Church of the Intercession

550 West 155th Street,
at Broadway
(212) 283-6200

Designated landmark

No church in Manhattan has a more expansive front yard than Intercession, set in the 24-acre Trinity Cemetery, the only one on the island that is still in use. Resting here in peace are John James Audubon, who lived nearby, and Clement Clarke Moore, whose grave is visited each Christmas in a procession commemeorating "A Visit from St. Nicholas."

The cemetery offers a verdant setting for this glorious Gothic church, built from 1911 to 1914, whose strong verticality and assertive massing recall the New South Reformed Church (now Park Avenue Christian Church). Both were the work of Bertram Grosvenor Goodhue, who is himself entombed at Intercession.

The congregation dates to 1847, when this neighborhood was a rural suburb called Carmansville. Trinity Church, no longer able to bury its dead in the Wall Street graveyard, had established a cemetery nearby four years earlier, presciently setting aside a portion of the acreage for a chapel. With the coming of the subway, the population of this once-remote outpost exploded, taxing Intercession's resources. The church did not have the money to build a new sanctuary and so turned to Old Trinity. Intercession was made a chapel of Trinity parish in 1908 and the mother congregation undertook the construction of Goodhue's cathedral-like church.

Intercession regained its independence in 1976. It drew citywide notice in 1989 when one of its parishioners, David N. Dinkins, became the first black mayor of New York City. His impending inauguration was celebrated here at a service with Archbishop Desmond M. Tutu of South Africa, the Rev. Jesse Jackson and a thousand other well-wishers. Intercession was also an important force in the neighborhood under the Rev. Canon Frederick B. Williams, a leader in the ecumenical housing program known as Harlem Churches for Community Improvement.

With 5,000 to 6,000 people using the church every week, the wear and tear on the physical plant had grown more than evident by the late 1990s, when a restoration project, designed by Jan Hird Pokorny, was undertaken.

On Sunday a low Mass begins at 8 a.m., solemn high Mass at 10 a.m., Spanish Mass at 12:30 p.m. and a Mass in the Igbo rite, as celebrated in Nigeria, at 2:30 p.m. Bilingual Masses are also celebrated.

Church of Jesus Christ of Latter-day Saints

1815 Riverside Drive, at Payson Avenue
(212) 567-3321 or
(212) 567-3351 (Spanish)
www.lds.org

The first church of the new millennium, at the foot of Fort Tryon Park, recalls the 18th century, with a slender white steeple rising over nearby rooftops from a sturdy red-brick base. But it actually represents something modern: energetic missionary work in Latino and black neighborhoods by the Church of Jesus Christ of Latter-day Saints, known to all but its adherents as the Mormon church. The church is also planning a new building at 56 West 129th Street in central Harlem.

This complex, designed by Frank Fernandez, has a 258-person chapel adjoining a combination cultural center and basketball court—"slam-dunk salvation," Juan Gonzalez wrote approvingly in the *Daily News*.

The chapel opened in March 2000 and holds Sunday services.

Masjid Malcolm Shabazz

102 West 116th Street,
at Malcolm X Boulevard
(212) 662-2201
e-mail: msmosque@aol.com

A startlingly plump dome on the Harlem skyline marks the masjid, or mosque, where El-Hajj Malik El-Shabazz—Malcolm X—once ministered.

Founded in 1946 at the Harlem Y.M.C.A. as Temple Seven of the Nation of Islam (Temple One was in Detroit), this mosque was just a storefront in 1954 when Elijah Muhammad named Malcolm its minister. "One bus couldn't have been filled with the Muslims in New York City," he recalled to Alex Haley in *The Autobiography of Malcolm X*. "Black Christians we 'fished' to our Temple were conditioned, I found, by the very shock I could give them about what had been happening to them while they worshiped a blond, blue-eyed God." It was at Temple Seven that Malcolm met Sister Betty X, whom he wed in 1958.

Splitting from Elijah Muhammad in 1964, Malcolm opened the Muslim Mosque at the Hotel Theresa. He was succeeded at Temple Seven by Louis X, later known as Minister Louis Farrakhan. The 116th Street building was destroyed by a dynamite blast following Malcolm's assassination in 1965, but was rebuilt five years later, to designs by Sabbath Brown.

Under Imam Ali Rashid, the mosque was renamed in 1976 and is now used by orthodox Sunni Muslims. Another Mosque Number Seven, at 106 West 127th Street, serves the Nation of Islam that was established by Farrakhan in 1978.

Since 1993 this masjid has been led by Imam Izak-El Mu'eed Pasha, who has raised its profile considerably in the broader community. It sponsored the new 11-story Renaissance Plaza apartment and retail development diagonally across the avenue. It is also expanding its school and developing a foster-care center. Eight thousand worshipers now attend services here.

Anyone wishing to visit the mosque or attend a service (Friday from 1 to 2:30 p.m.) should call (212) 662-2200. No photography or taping is permitted, and there is a dress code.

Mother A.M.E. Zion Church

140 West 137th Street,
near Adam Clayton Powell Jr. Boulevard
(212) 234-1545
motherafricanmethodistezchurch.com

Designated landmark

Behind a crisply articulated Collegiate Gothic façade lies the rich
spiritual story of the oldest black church in New York, associated
over time with Duke Ellington, Paul Robeson, Sojourner Truth, Harriet
Tubman and Madame C.J. Walker, among others.

Mother African Methodist Episcopal Zion
Church is the founding congregation (Mother)
of a denomination led by the sons and daugh-
ters of Africa, guided by Wesleyan (Methodist)
principles and supervised by bishops
(Episcopal). Zion, referring to the church of
God, distinguishes this from other A.M.E. bodies.

It was founded in 1796 by James Varick,
Peter Williams and others who were unhappy
with the discriminatory practices at the John
Street Methodist Church, where black members
were made to wait for communion until white members had partaken.

Varick became the first bishop of the denomination and his remains
are preserved in a crypt at this church. Mother Zion built a sanctuary in
1800 at Church and Leonard Streets, a spot still marked by a bronze
tablet set into the sidewalk. Sojourner Truth joined the church while it was
there. In the middle of the 19th century, the denomination came to be
known as the Freedom Church for its key role in the Underground
Railroad. Another A.M.E. Zion church, built in 1853, served the settlement known as Seneca Village, in what is now Central Park.

Mother Zion had a church on Bleecker Street beginning in 1864,
only two blocks from Abyssinian, which was then on Waverly Place.
Mother Zion then moved to West 89th Street and to West 136th Street
before settling in its present home.

The present church was designed by George Washington Foster Jr.,
the pioneering black architect who also collaborated with Vertner Tandy
on St. Philip's. It was built from 1923 to 1925, with room for 2,300 worshipers. More than twice that number attended the funeral in 1976 of
Paul Robeson, the actor, singer and social activist, whose brother, the Rev.
Benjamin C. Robeson, was the pastor at Mother Zion for four decades.

**Visitors are welcome at the 11 a.m. Sunday service but are asked to
stay throughout or to leave quietly during the meditation hymn.**

Church of Our Lady of Lourdes

467 West 142nd Street,
near Amsterdam Avenue
(212) 862-4380

Designated landmark

Looking more like a palazzo on the Grand Canal—check out those ebullient two-toned arches—than a parish church in Harlem, Our Lady of Lourdes offers many surprises to the attentive visitor.

Built from 1902 to 1904, it is a marvelous, recycled hybrid, beginning with the pedestals flanking the stairway, which come from the Fifth Avenue mansion of A. T. Stewart, the dry-goods king of the mid-19th century. The main façade incorporates much of the material and aesthetic spirit of the National Academy of Design, a Venetian Gothic structure built in 1865 at Park Avenue South and East 23rd Street.

Inside is St. Patrick's Cathedral. Literally. Stained-glass windows and other architectural elements removed from the east end of the cathedral to permit the addition of the Lady Chapel were brought

here. The architect who threaded all these elements together, Cornelius O'Reilly, died after falling off a ladder while inspecting the church.

Our Lady of Lourdes serves a most diverse population, including African-Americans, Dominicans, Ecuadoreans, Eritreans and Mexicans.

Sunday Masses are celebrated in English at 7:30 and 10 a.m.; in Spanish at 8:45 a.m., 12 noon and 1:15 p.m. Weekday Masses are in English at 9 a.m. and Spanish at 7:30 p.m.

St. Cecilia's Church

120 East 106th Street,
near Lexington Avenue
(212) 534-1350
www.east-harlem.com/stcecili.htm

Designated landmark

Camels, donkeys and sheep are not the sort of traffic one expects on East 106th Street, but each year on Jan. 6 they parade by this big Roman Catholic church on Three Kings' Day, a holiday so significant in Hispanic culture that it is called the second Christmas. St. Cecilia's is a focal point of life in El Barrio at other times as well. Sister Regina Burns established a pioneering AIDS ministry here in 1989. In 1998 Cardinal John J. O'Connor helped celebrate the parish's 125th anniversary, drawing crowds that filled the balconies in this vast sanctuary. The rugged, red-brick Romanesque structure was built from 1883 to 1887 to designs by Napoleon Le Brun & Sons. From the façade, a terra-cotta relief of St. Cecilia herself, playing an organ, looks out over the streets of East Harlem.

Sunday Masses are celebrated in Spanish at 8 and 11:30 a.m. and in English at 9:45 a.m. There is an English vigil Mass Saturday at 5:30. Daily Masses are in Spanish at 8:15 a.m. and in English at 7 a.m. and 12:10 p.m.

Shrine of
St. Frances
Xavier Cabrini

701 Fort Washington Avenue,
at West 190th Street
(212) 923-3536
www.cabrinishrineny.org

Quite truly larger than life, a two-story-high stained-glass image of Mother Cabrini, the patron of immigrants and the first American citizen to be made a saint, overlooks the Hudson River from a stunning spot just south of the Cloisters. But what is she doing here?

Frances Xavier Cabrini was born in 1850 in Lombardy. She founded the Missionary Sisters of the Sacred Heart of Jesus in 1880 to care for poor children. Pope Leo XIII sent her to New York nine years later with a small group of sisters, to help Italian immigrants. Despite initial misgivings on the part of the Catholic hierarchy, Mother Cabrini was able to establish a number of vital institutions, including Columbus Hospital, now Cabrini Medical Center.

She also bought property in Washington Heights from C.K.G. Billings, whose estate would later became part of Fort Tryon Park, and established her headquarters in the Sacred Heart Villa at 701 Fort Washington Avenue, where Mother Cabrini High School now stands. (*That's* what she's doing here.)

Her calling took her back and forth to Europe, throughout Central and South America and around the United States, where she established 67 schools, hospitals and orphanages. She died in Chicago in 1917. After the high school was built, Mother Cabrini's remains were returned to Washington Heights and enshrined. She was canonized in 1946 by Pope Pius XII.

Her shrine chapel, designed by De Sina & Pellegrino, was completed in 1960. The floor plan is a parabolic arch, with mosaics depicting Mother Cabrini's life wrapping around an altar in which a wax effigy is displayed for veneration.

The shrine is open every day from 9 a.m. to 4:30 p.m. Masses are at 9 and 11 a.m. on Sunday and 7 a.m., Monday to Friday. From Memorial Day to Labor Day, the shrine is open until 7 p.m. There are no Masses during the week. There is a gift shop.

St. Martin's Church

230 Malcolm X Boulevard,
at West 122nd Street
(212) 534-4531

Designated landmark

Manhattan has many bell towers, but only a few carillons. The one at Riverside Church was a Rockefeller gift. The one at St. Martin's Episcopal was bought by the parishioners with their very hard-earned money. They are proudly called the "poor people's bells" by the Rev. David Johnson, whose father, the Rev. John Howard Johnson, founded this parish in 1928.

The congregation first met in and eventually took over a sanctuary built as the Church of the Holy Trinity. Designed by William A. Potter and completed in 1888, it is the closest thing Manhattan has to the ruggedly exuberant Romanesque style of Henry Hobson Richardson, embodied by Trinity Church in Boston.

The Holy Trinity congregation moved far uptown to Inwood, leaving its church to St. Martin's, which was made a full-fledged parish in 1940 and counted the artist Romare Bearden among its members.

In 1949 St. Martin's bought a 42-bell carillon from the Van Bergen foundry in the Netherlands. The extraordinary nature of this acquisition was underscored three years later, when Queen Juliana of the Netherlands came to visit the church. By the end of the 1990s, however, for want of a carilloneur and the wherewithal to keep the tower in good repair, the bells went silent—at least temporarily—while money was being raised for their restoration.

Communion services are at 8 and 9 a.m. on Sunday and 9:30 a.m. on Thursday. Morning prayer and litany with sermon are on Sunday at 11 a.m.

St. Philip's Church

214 West 134th Street,
near Adam Clayton Powell Jr. Boulevard
(212) 862-4940

Designated landmark

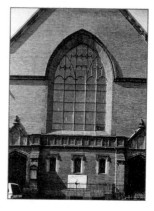

Abyssinian Baptist is widely thought of as synonymous with black Harlem. But it was venerable St. Philip's Episcopal that really led the exodus uptown in 1911. "As the emergence of the year's first crocus announces that spring is on its way, so did the arrival of so important a church as St. Philip's signify that Harlem was sure to be the next major settlement of blacks in Manhattan," Jervis Anderson wrote in *This Was Harlem.*

Even without that distinction, St. Philip's would be every bit a landmark as the oldest black Episcopal congregation in New York and, in its day, one of the largest and most influential parishes of any color. It grew out of the African Episcopal Catechetical Institution and was designated New York's tenth parish in 1818. It built its own church on Centre Street, under Peter Williams Jr., the first African-American to be ordained in the Episcopal church. When mobs sacked the church in 1839, the bishop of New York did not denounce the desecration but instead called on Williams to resign from the Anti-Slavery Society.

St. Philip's church on Mulberry Street was used as a barracks during the Civil War Draft Riots. The Rev. Hutchens Chew Bishop moved the parish to a former Presbyterian church on West 25th Street, just a block away from Bethel A.M.E. By 1909 Bishop was planning a church in Harlem.

This neo-Gothic sanctuary was designed by two pioneering African-American architects, Vertner W. Tandy and George Washington Foster Jr., who also designed Mother A.M.E. Zion Church. St. Philip's presents a strikingly simple gabled façade of Roman brick, dominated by a Perpendicular-style tracery window. The reredos, or altar screen, came from the 25th Street church. The chancel ceiling collapsed in 1996, and the church enlisted Ed Kamper to direct the restoration of its slate roof.

St. Philip's has counted as members or worshipers W.E.B. Dubois, Langston Hughes and Thurgood Marshall. The Archbishop of Canterbury, spiritual leader of the Anglican Communion, visited in 1981 and presented the Order of the Cross of St. Augustine to the Rev. M. Moran Weston. During Weston's long tenure, St. Philip's developed five nonprofit housing projects, including homes for the elderly and the mentally ill, and a child development and day-care center.

There are two services at St. Philip's each Sunday: the Family Eucharist at 9 a.m. and Holy Eucharist at 11. Another Holy Eucharist service is conducted on Wednesday at 6 p.m.

Church of St. Thomas the Apostle

260 West 118th Street, near St. Nicholas Avenue (212) 662-2693

Rising over the tough edges of St. Nicholas Avenue like a fantastic lace scrim, this Roman Catholic church is even more awesome inside, with stained-glass windows that form virtual walls of color, interspersed with elaborate stations of the cross, under a spidery

fan-vaulted ceiling almost worthy of Kings College Chapel in Cambridge. St. Thomas the Apostle not only defies expectation, it has also defied extinction, having been rescued in 1979 by the Salesians of Don Bosco, a religious order that emphasizes working with youth. The parish was founded in 1889 and built this church in 1907, to designs by Thomas H. Poole. Hulan E. Jack, the first black borough president of Manhattan, was buried from here in 1986.

The only time the glorious main sanctuary is open is for the 10:15 a.m. Mass on Sunday. All other services, including the daily 8 a.m. Mass, are held in the rectory chapel.

First Spanish United Methodist Church
1791 Lexington Avenue, at East 111th Street

This modest A-frame sanctuary was called the "People's Church" during an 11-day occupation by the Young Lords Organization, a militant Puerto Rican group, at the end of 1969. The incident is remembered as a milestone in the raising of political consciousness in El Barrio.

Fort Washington Presbyterian Church
21 Wadsworth Avenue, at West 174th Street

Looking very much as if it would be at home in London, this overscaled Georgian church with bell tower was designed by Carrère & Hastings and built in 1914.

Metropolitan Baptist Church
151 West 128th Street, at Adam Clayton Powell Jr. Boulevard
Designated landmark

A great conical roof, recalling the shingle-style "cottages" of the upper crust, distinguishes this landmark, built from 1884 to 1890. The architect was John R. Thomas, followed by Richard R. Davis.

Mount Olivet Baptist Church
201 Malcolm X Boulevard, at West 120th Street
Within a historic district

Its monumental colonnade qualifies it as perhaps the finest single example of the neoclassical synagogue. It was designed as Temple Israel in 1907 by the architect of Shearith Israel, Arnold W. Brunner.

Church of St. Aloysius
209 West 132nd Street, near Adam Clayton Powell Jr. Boulevard.

A startlingly shimmering, almost opalescent façade of greens and purples, designed in 1904 by the firm of W. W. Renwick. It is the oldest black Roman Catholic church in Harlem.

St. Andrew's Church
2067 Fifth Avenue, at East 127th Street
Designated landmark

Most congregations simply leave their old buildings behind when they move. This Episcopalian group disassembled its Victorian Gothic sanctuary, completed in 1873 to designs by Henry M. Congdon, and moved it two and a half blocks to this site in 1890.

United Church
4140 Broadway, at West 175th Street

Long associated with the charismatic Reverend Ike (the Rev. Frederick J. Eikerenkoetter II), this was built in 1930 as the Loew's 175th Street Theater by Thomas W. Lamb, in what can only be described as the Byzantine-Romanesque-Indo-Sino-Moorish-Persian-Eclectic-Rococo-Deco style.

A

B

I

J

K

N

O

P

Q

R

Saint

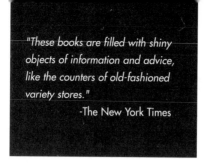

Welcome to
City & Company Guidebooks
for New Yorkers
and Their Friends

NEW YORK'S
100 BEST
LITTLE PLACES TO SHOP

In this shopper's paradise, you'll find 100 one-of-a-kind chic little boutiques and unique specialty stores, quirky and diverse as the city itself. SECOND EDITION

Eve Claxton
160 pp 1–88549–70–7 $15

NEW YORK'S
60 BEST
WONDERFUL LITTLE HOTELS

This bestselling book to New York's growing number of boutique hotels, inns, and B&Bs covers the hip to homey, the luxurious to spare and all the stylish new favorites in town. SECOND EDITION

Allen Sperry
160 pp 1–885492–81–2 $15

NEW YORK'S
50 BEST
PLACES TO HAVE BRUNCH

Venture beyond your neighborhood standbys and discover the best
spots in town (and their signature dishes). With suggestions on
where to go afterward for the perfect weekend in New York.

Ann Volkwein & Jason Nixon
128 pp 1–885492–69–3 $12

NEW YORK'S
75 BEST
NIGHTS OUT

Tour the great bars, lounges, performance spaces, restaurants, live
music venues, dance clubs and you'll discover the best good times
the city can offer. SECOND EDITION

Angela Tribelli
112 pp 1–885492–86–3 $12

NEW YORK'S
NEW & AVANT-GARDE
ART GALLERIES

You'll be able to navigate the city's modern and cutting edge art galleries with this insider's guide to a constantly changing scene, filled
with intellecutal stimuation, surprise and fun.

Barbara Stone
128 pp 1–885492–82–0 $14

NEW YORK'S
50 BEST
PLACES TO FIND PEACE
AND QUIET

"If you're at wit's end and frantic for tranquility, relax...you can buy
a sweet little book...." —*The New York Times*.
Now with 10 additional locations. SECOND EDITION

Allan Ishac
128 pp. 1–885492–52–9 $12

CITY WEDDING:
**A Guide
to the Best Bridal
Resources
in New York,
Long Island,
Westchester,
New Jersey
and Connecticut**

The only all-in-one resource guide to planning a wedding-to-remember in the metropolitan area. It covers wedding planners and consultants, reception locations, bridal gowns, catering, invitations, florists, cakes, bands, hotography, gift registries and more.

Joan Hamburg
170 pp. 1-885492-89-8 $17.95

NEW YORK'S 50 BEST PLACES TO TAKE CHILDREN

Here's a guaranteed good time for kids ages 1-12 and for their parents, grandparents, and teachers too. These unusual spots veer off the beaten path and note the coolest part of each site.

Allan Ishac
128 pp 1–885492–30–8 $12

HEAVENLY WEEKENDS:
Travel Without a Car

These 52 daytrips, overnight and weekend getaways in New York, New Jersey, Connecticut and Pennsylvania are all accessible by train and bus. Organized by distance from the city, one to four hours away, with detailed travel instructions and suggestions for eating and staying.

Susan Clemett and Gena Vandestienne
208 pp 1-885492-59-6 $14.95

THE NEW ULTRA COOL PARENTS GUIDE TO ALL OF NEW YORK:

Excursions & Activities In & Around Our City that Your Children Will Love and You Won't Think are Too Bad Either

"Tantalizing details on stuff you can't find in other guide books," wrote *New York* magazine. *The New York Times* said, "the activities they discuss are chosen as much for the pleasure of parents as children."

Alfred Gingold and Helen Rogan
144 pp. 1–885492–76-6 $14.95

NEW YORK'S 50 BEST MUSEUMS FOR COOL PARENTS AND THEIR KIDS

Visiting museums with your children can be fun. Really! The authors of *The Cool Parents Guide to All of New York* offer tips on tackling the immense institutions to little gems, from the tried and true to the unfamiliar and the slightly weird.

Alfred Gingold and Helen Rogan
160 pp 1–88549–83-9 $14

NEW YORK'S 50 BEST PLACES TO DISCOVER AND ENJOY IN CENTRAL PARK

An entertaining and detailed user's guide to the 843 acres of beauty and wonder that are Central Park by the president of the Central Park Conservancy and Park planner and architect.

Karen Putnam and Marianne Cramer,
Central Park Conservancy 144 pp 1–885492–64–2 $12

Guides to the Best of New York

City Baby:
A Resource for NY Parents $15.95

City Wedding:
A Guide to the Best Bridal Resources $17.95

The Food Lover's Guide
to the Best Ethnic Eating in New York $14.95

Hampton's Survival Guide $17.95

Heavenly Weekends:
Travel Without a Car $14.95

How to Live the Good Life
in New York $20.00

New York's New
& Avant-Garde Art Galleries $14.00

New York's 50 Best
Art in Public Places $12.00

New York's 50 Best
Places to Go Birding $15.00

New York's 50 Best
Bookstores for Booklovers $12.00

New York's 50 Best
Places to Have Brunch $12.00

New York's 50 Best
Places to Discover and Enjoy
in Central Park $12.00

New York's 50 Best
Places to Take Children $12.00

New York's 60 Best
Wonderful Little Hotels $15.00

New York's 75 Best
Nights Out $12.00

New York's 50 Best
Places to Have a Kid's Party $12.00

New York's 50 Best
Museums for Cool Parents
and Their Kids $14.00

New York's 50 Best
Places to Find Peace & Quiet $12.00

New York's 100 Best
Little Places to Shop $15.00

New York's 100 Best
Party Places $14.00

Brooklyn's Best:
Happy Wandering
in the Borough of Kings $14.00

You can find our books at your local bookstore,
through booksellers on the web,
or by contacting
City & Company 22 West 23rd Street
New York, NY 10010
tel: 212.366.1988   fax: 212.242.0415
e-mail: cityco@mindspring.com
www.cityandcompany.com

City & Company guides
can be used as corporate gifts or promotions.
Special editions can be created to specification.
Please write to:
Premium Marketing, City & Company,
22 West 23rd Street, New York, NY 10010

About the Authors

David W. Dunlap covers the built environment—architecture, construction, neighborhood development and historical landmarks—for *The New York Times*, where he has worked since 1975. He is the author and photographer of *On Broadway: A Journey Uptown Over Time* (Rizzoli International Publications, 1990) and the photographer of *The City Observed: New York* by Paul Goldberger (Random House, 1979).

Joseph J. Vecchione is an editor with *The New York Times*.